CHICAGO PUBLIC LIBRARY
SULZER REGIONAL
4455 N. LINCOLN
CHICAGO, IL 60625

JUV/
KF
228
.C78
F75
2005
SULZER   Cruzan v. Missouri and the right to die

MAR   2006

Debating Supreme Court Decisions

Cruzan v. Missouri and the Right to Die Debate

Debating Supreme Court Decisions

Ron Fridell

Enslow Publishers, Inc.
40 Industrial Road   PO Box 38
Box 398   Aldershot
Berkeley Heights, NJ 07922   Hants GU12 6BP
USA   UK
http://www.enslow.com

Copyright © 2005 by Ron Fridell

All rights reserved.

No part of this book may be reproduced by any means without the written permission of the publisher.

Library of Congress Cataloging-in-Publication Data

Fridell, Ron.
　　Cruzan v. Missouri and the right to die debate : debating Supreme Court decisions / Ron Fridell.— 1st ed.
　　　　p. cm. — (Debating Supreme Court decisions)
　　Includes bibliographical references and index.
　　ISBN 0-7660-2356-7
　　1. Cruzan, Nancy—Trials, litigation, etc.—Juvenile literature. 2. Cruzan, Joe—Trials, litigation, etc.—Juvenile literature. 3. Right to die—Law and legislation—United States.—Juvenile literature. I. Title. II. Series.
KF228.C78F75 2005
344.7304'197—dc22

　　　　　　　　　　　　　　　　2004020028

Printed in the United States of America

10 9 8 7 6 5 4 3 2 1

To Our Readers: We have done our best to make sure that all Internet Addresses in this book were active and appropriate when we went to press. However, the author and publisher have no control over and assume no liability for the material available on those Internet sites or on other Web sites they may link to. Any comments or suggestions can be sent by e-mail to comments@enslow.com or to the address on the back cover.

Illustration Credits: Illustration Credits: All photographs are from AP/Wide World, except for the following: Bob Dougherty/Collection of the Supreme Court of the United States, p. 82; Getty Images, p. 12; Hemera Image Express, p. 2.

Cover Illustrations: Background, Artville; photographs, AP/Wide World.

Contents

1. Legal Questions:
   The Case of Elizabeth Bouvia 5
2. The Changing Face of Death 17
3. Through Supporters' Eyes 26
4. Through Opponents' Eyes 37
5. Right to Die Laws 52
6. Lower Court Cases 63
7. U.S. Supreme Court Cases 76
8. The Issues Today 90
9. Moot Court: Your Turn to Debate 97

   Questions for Discussion 104
   Chronology 106
   Chapter Notes 111
   Glossary 119
   Further Reading 123
   Internet Addresses 124
   Index 125

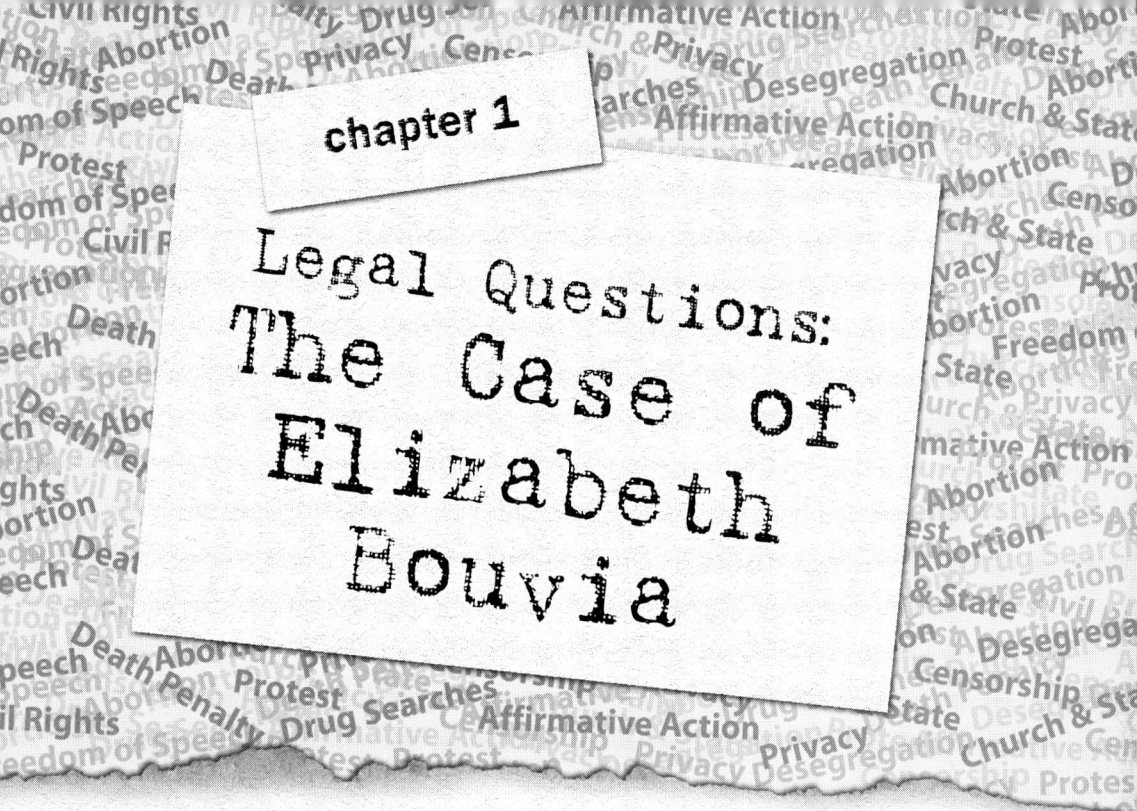

chapter 1
Legal Questions: The Case of Elizabeth Bouvia

Being alive is a wonderful thing, but nobody lives forever. Sooner or later everyone dies. But when, where, how? Imagine planning the details of your own death in advance. Who in the world would do such a thing?

Elizabeth Bouvia was a brave, bright, determined young woman. She had earned a college degree despite being born with a crippling disease. Cerebral palsy had severely damaged her central nervous system. She was unable to move by herself. Family and friends had to bathe her and dress her and take her to the toilet. She could swallow food on her own, but someone else had to spoon it into her mouth. Every day of her life was a painful struggle, Bouvia said.

Finally, she could not take the struggle any longer.

Cruzan v. Missouri and the Right to Die Debate

"You can only fight for so long. It's a struggle for a person like me to live and a struggle to die," she said. "It is more of a struggle to live than die. Death is letting go of all burdens."[1]

Elizabeth Bouvia was twenty-six in 1983 when she decided to take her own life. But now she faced a new set of obstacles. Without freedom of movement, unassisted suicide was impossible. "If I really could, I would go out there and kill myself," she said. "But I can't. I physically can't."[2]

Someone would have to assist her. But who? Could a physician provide her with a lethal dose of drugs? Not without committing a crime. Suicide itself was not against the law, but helping someone else commit suicide was. And that included physician-assisted suicide. But even if Bouvia could get the deadly drugs, someone else would have to place them in her mouth for her to swallow. And that would be active euthanasia, an even more serious crime.

Then what could Bouvia do? She considered the possibilities and devised a plan to end her life as comfortably and painlessly as possible. When Elizabeth Bouvia made her plan, she was struggling to exercise what she believed was her right to die.

What Is the Right to Die?

This may sound like a strange kind of "right" to fight for, since we all must die one day. What the

Legal Questions: The Case of Elizabeth Bouvia

"right to die" means is the legal, constitutional right to choose when, where, and how you will die. But does such a legal right really exist for anyone under any circumstances? Is this an absolute right, without limits? As we shall see, there are limits to the right to die, and those limits are part of an intense legal debate.

Many people who attempt to exercise this right are patients in a hospital or nursing home who have been told that they are terminally ill—that they have less than six months to live. If not for special life-support equipment and medicines, they would die in a matter of days or weeks. These terminally ill patients want physicians to withhold this special treatment so that they may die a natural death.

Others, like Elizabeth Bouvia, are severely disabled. They are not terminally ill; they may live on for many years. But in their eyes, their quality of life is so poor that they would rather not be alive. To them, their lives are no longer worth living. They wish to die peacefully, assisted by physicians or other health-care workers.

Bouvia had this wish in mind when she put her plan into action. She had herself taken to California's Riverside General Hospital. Once she was checked in, she refused all food and water. Within two weeks she would starve herself to death. Meanwhile, the hospital staff would keep her as comfortable as possible, giving her drugs to ease her pain. That was her plan.

Not a Simple Matter

Elizabeth Bouvia believed that she had the legal right to choose to die, and she expected the hospital staff to help her exercise this right. But the staff saw things differently. They were running an institution dedicated to helping patients live, not die. They could not stand back and allow a patient to starve to death while in their care.

But their patient absolutely refused to swallow the food they spooned into her mouth, so they had to resort to force-feeding. A witness described the gruesome scene: "Four or more 'attendants' wrestle her from her bed in the morning and restrain her while a nasogastric [feeding] tube is rudely forced through her nose and into her stomach."[3]

So Bouvia sued the hospital staff. She asked the court to force the staff to halt the feedings and honor her legal right to die. At this point, the American Civil Liberties Union (ACLU) stepped in. The ACLU is a national organization dedicated to preserving an individual's legal rights and liberties. The ACLU agreed with Bouvia. They believed the hospital must honor her request to refuse medical treatment. She could not afford to hire legal help for a long court battle, so the ACLU provided her an attorney free of charge.

Bouvia's Trials

During the next three years, Elizabeth Bouvia and her attorney fought her case in the California courts. First, a trial court denied her request. The court ruled that it amounted to "an attempt to commit suicide with the state's help rather than a bona fide [genuine] exercise of her right to refuse medical treatment."[4]

Bouvia and her attorney appealed this 1983 decision to a higher court. Appeals courts review lower court cases to see whether they were decided fairly and accurately. An appeals court may reverse a lower court's decision.

In 1986, the California Court of Appeal, Second Appellate District, gave its decision in *Bouvia* v. *Superior Court*. In the ruling, written by Judge Beach, the court stated that both sides had strong points in their favor. The hospital had a genuine interest in preserving life and preventing suicide. Yet the patient, who was not terminally ill, was asking to commit suicide with the hospital's help.

However, the judge wrote,

> The right to refuse medical treatment is . . . recognized as a part of the right of privacy protected by both the state and federal constitutions. . . . It is a moral and philosophical decision that, being a competent adult, is [Bouvia's] alone.[5]

By the term "competent," Judge Beach meant

that Bouvia had the mental capacity to make decisions about life and death for herself.

And so the California appeals court reversed the trial court's decision. It granted Bouvia's request that the hospital staff remove the feeding tube and allow her to die.

Questions Raised

The *Bouvia* appeals court ruling answered the following legal questions:

- Was Elizabeth Bouvia herself free to end her life? Yes, she was.
- Must the staff of physicians and nurses at Riverside General Hospital allow her to starve herself to death under their care? Yes, they must.

But the *Bouvia* ruling also raised other legal questions.

The Other Side

The troubling legal questions raised by *Bouvia v. Superior Court* are still being hotly debated in courts of law in the United States. They represent one side of the right to die controversy. This is the side involving medical patients who are competent, who can make life-and-death decisions for themselves.

The other side concerns medical patients who are not competent. Some of these patients are infants who are severely handicapped or adults

Legal Questions: The Case of Elizabeth Bouvia

Legal Questions Raised by *Bouvia v. Superior Court* (1986)

◆ When does a competent medical patient have the right to choose to die?

◆ When, if ever, should physicians or other health-care workers help a competent patient die?

◆ Who should make these decisions? The patient? The state? The courts?

who are severely mentally ill or retarded. Some are patients who have suffered severe brain damage that has left them in a persistent vegetative state (PVS).

At any one time, there are an estimated 10,000 PVS patients in the United States.[6] Some were in automobile accidents. Others had strokes or heart attacks. They are technically alive but permanently unconscious and unaware of their surroundings. Their hearts beat and their lungs breathe, but their brains have stopped thinking. Most of these PVS patients will never again be conscious, though a few may regain some degree of awareness. Feeding tubes and other life-support equipment keep them technically alive. If this technology is withdrawn, they will die.

The Case of Nancy Cruzan

Nancy Cruzan was a PVS patient. She was twenty-five years old in 1983 when an automobile accident left her in a persistent vegetative state. She was being cared for in a Missouri nursing home. She could breathe for herself but could not swallow. A tube dripped food and water into her stomach to keep her alive.

Should she continue living in this way? Nancy was not competent to decide, but her parents believed they knew what she would want. If only Nancy could be brought back to consciousness for

Nancy Cruzan, who was in a persistent vegetative state following a car accident, was the center of a right to die case that went to the Supreme Court.

Legal Questions: The Case of Elizabeth Bouvia

a moment, they thought, she would ask to be allowed to die.

As Nancy's guardians, her parents were legally responsible for her care. Now they wanted to act as her surrogates, to speak for her. This is known as the doctrine of substituted judgment. The guardians' judgment is substituted for the incompetent patient's wishes.

So Nancy's parents asked the staff to remove the feeding tube. But the staff refused, so the Cruzans and their attorney filed a lawsuit. They sued the Missouri state government, which was paying for Nancy's care, along with the nursing home. The Cruzans lost the case, but that did not stop them. They filed a petition with a Missouri appeals court.

More Questions Raised

The Cruzans lost in the first appeals court, too. But they went on appealing the decision to higher appeals courts until, in 1990, the case reached the highest appeals court in the nation, the U.S. Supreme Court. Its decision is final. The case was known as *In re Cruzan*. ("In re" stands for "In the matter of.") This book will refer to the case by its more familiar name, *Cruzan v. Missouri*, which is short for *Cruzan v. Director, Missouri Department of Health*. This is the name the case was given in the lower courts, before it reached the U.S. Supreme Court.

In an appeals case, the opposing parties are known as the petitioner and the respondent. The petitioner, who lost the lower court case, asks the appeals court to reverse that decision. The respondent, who won the lower court case, asks that the decision stand as is.

The attorneys who argued the case for the petitioners and respondents all had strong points in their favor. The petitioners—the Cruzans—claimed that Nancy's right to refuse medical treatment and be allowed to die was protected by two separate constitutional rights. One was the right to privacy. The state had no right to decide Nancy's private fate, the Cruzans said. The other was the right to freedom from cruel and unusual punishment, as guaranteed in the Eighth Amendment and applied to the states through the Fourteenth Amendment. The nursing home was cruelly punishing Nancy, forcing her to live on in a hopelessly unconscious condition, the Cruzans insisted.

The respondents, on the other hand, had strong reasons for keeping Nancy alive. The nursing home staff had a long-standing duty to help make patients better and never to harm them. And the state of Missouri had a duty to preserve and protect the lives of its citizens.

After weighing all these points carefully, the U.S.

Legal Questions: The Case of Elizabeth Bouvia

Supreme Court decided in favor of the respondents. The nursing home did not have to remove the feeding tube. Nancy Cruzan would be kept alive.

Like *Bouvia*, the *Cruzan* ruling raised troubling legal questions about a person's right to choose to die.

Legal Questions Raised by *Cruzan v. Missouri* (1990)

- When, if ever, does a guardian have the right to choose death for an incompetent patient?
- Should the state insist on prolonging life by artificial means even when there is no hope of recovery?
- Do patients, competent or incompetent, have a constitutionally protected right to choose to die?

The troubling legal questions raised by the *Bouvia* and *Cruzan* rulings are addressed every day in courts, universities, churches, hospitals, and the media. Physicians and philosophers puzzle over them. Lawyers debate them in courtrooms, and politicians debate them in legislatures.

This book will look closely at the debate surrounding legal questions about the right to choose

Cruzan v. Missouri and the Right to Die Debate

to die. *Cruzan* v. *Missouri* will be covered in detail later on. We will also revisit *Bouvia* v. *Superior Court* to reveal the surprising events that followed that ruling.

We will examine these difficult questions, but we will not arrive at any final answers. When it comes to troubling questions of law, there can be no final answers. The next chapter explains why.

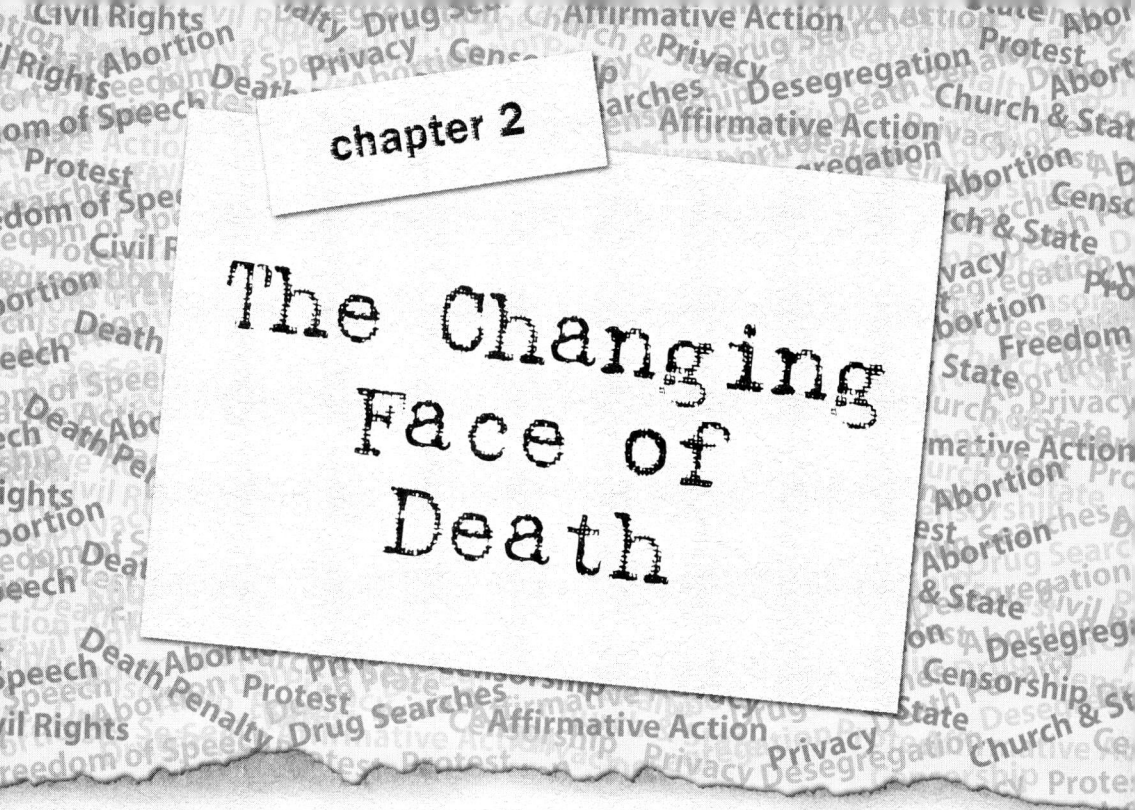

chapter 2
The Changing Face of Death

In 2003, a U.S. citizen could expect to live to age seventy-seven. But a century earlier, that age was only forty-seven. What are the reasons for this huge rise in life expectancy, the average number of years that people live?

Actually, many Americans lived to a ripe old age a century ago. But tens of thousands of infants and children died from infectious diseases. These infant deaths are what kept life expectancy so low. Epidemics of diphtheria, cholera, and influenza would come sweeping through villages and towns, taking many young lives suddenly.

People knew that germs caused these diseases, but they did not yet know how to stop them. These fatal diseases influenced people's view of death.

When one of these diseases took hold, there was nothing anyone could do. The patient's life was in God's hands, they believed. Doctors would therefore stop trying to save the lives of terminally ill patients. Instead, they would do all they could to make the patient's death as painless and comfortable as possible.

A New View of Death

As the nineteenth century drew to a close, scientists began conquering these fatal diseases, one by one. They found that vaccines, which are dead or weakened forms of disease-causing bacteria or viruses, could prevent them. By 1890, scientists had found a vaccine for diphtheria. More vaccines for other fatal diseases followed, including polio. In 1928, research scientist Alexander Fleming developed penicillin, a powerful new antibiotic that worked against scarlet fever and pneumonia. Later, other scientists developed antibiotics that worked against other fatal diseases. Today, nearly all these infectious diseases have been conquered. Infants are vaccinated against them, and cases of diphtheria and most other infectious diseases in the United States are rare.

In addition to cures, scientists developed effective techniques for repairing and replacing damaged organs. The first successful human

The Changing Face of Death

organ transplant was performed in 1954. Today, patients can get new hearts, new livers, new lungs.

Scientists also developed life-support technologies for keeping severely disabled and dying people alive over long periods of time. Respirator machines could breathe for people unable to breathe for themselves. Special tubes could deliver food and water to people unable to swallow.

These medical innovations changed people's attitudes toward death. Fewer people saw their fate as being beyond their control, and many felt it rested firmly in the hands of science.

Patients and Privacy

Patients also developed a new view of themselves. As a result, laws about medical matters changed. A landmark U.S. Supreme Court case from 1891 shows these changes at work.

The case was *Union Pacific Railway Company v. Botsford*. Clara Botsford was suing for physical injuries she had suffered while working for the railway. She wanted money as compensation for her injuries. Railway officials refused to pay unless she agreed to be examined by a doctor. During this examination, she would have to undress.

Clara Botsford refused. Undressing in front of a doctor would violate her right to privacy, she said. Ms. Botsford was demanding a right that would one day become a cornerstone in right to die cases: the right to refuse medical treatment.

The U.S. Supreme Court agreed with the lower court's ruling. Ms. Botsford need not be examined by a doctor against her will, since that would violate her right to personal privacy. The Court stated:

> No right is held more sacred, or is more carefully guarded by the common law, than the right of every individual to the possession and control of his own person, free from all restraint or interference of others, unless by clear and unquestionable authority of law.[1]

Patients' Rights

Botsford became a landmark case in U.S. Supreme Court history because it planted a seed that would grow through the years. That seed was personal

---

Significance of *Union Pacific Railway Company v. Botsford* (1891)

This landmark U.S. Supreme Court case established the following:

◇ Each person has certain rights when it comes to his or her own body.

◇ These include a patient's right to refuse medical treatment.

autonomy, the freedom to determine for ourselves what we will do and how we will behave.

No one is entirely autonomous, of course. We have rights to exercise, but we also have responsibilities to meet. When we break laws, we can expect to be punished. But people cannot be made to do certain things they do not wish to do, as *Botsford* established.

The ruling in a New York Court of Appeals case twenty-three years later proclaimed the principle of autonomy even more strongly. In a case entitled *Mary E. Schloendorff* v. *The Society of the New York Hospital* (1914), a patient named Mary Schloendorff consented to be examined for a brain tumor. While she was still under sedation from ether, a surgeon found a tumor and removed it—without first asking the patient's consent. As a result, Schloendorff claimed, she suffered intense pain and had to be operated on several more times. In the court's decision, Judge Benjamin Cardozo wrote:

> Every human being of adult years and sound mind has a right to determine what shall be done with his own body; and a surgeon who performs an operation without his patient's consent, commits an assault, for which he is liable in damages.[2]

As the twentieth century moved along, people demanded more personal autonomy. African Americans fought to end racial segregation, and women worked to gain equal rights with men. Medical patients also made demands. The U.S. Supreme Court ruling in *Roe* v. *Wade* (1973) dealt with a Texas law that outlawed medical abortion unless it was needed to save a mother's life. *Roe* struck this law down. In doing this, *Roe* also made abortion legal in all fifty states. Women everywhere now had the right to decide for themselves whether to have a physician end their pregnancy for any reason if the fetus was less than three months old. At three to six months of pregnancy, states could pass laws regulating abortion to safeguard women's health. In the last three months of pregnancy, states could pass laws forbidding abortion except to protect the life or health of the pregnant woman.

In *Botsford*, it was the right of the patient to refuse medical treatment. In *Roe*, it was the right

Significance of *Roe* v. *Wade* (1973)

This landmark U.S. Supreme Court case established the following:

⬥ The state has a genuine interest in protecting the health and safety of the pregnant woman and the potential human life within her.

⬥ However, these state interests do not extend to denying a woman her right to decide for herself whether to end a pregnancy.

of the patient to have an abortion. In both cases, the Court left it up to the patient to make decisions about medical treatment. As we shall see, both cases had a powerful influence on right to die cases to come.

The Right to Die Movement

Roe was part of a powerful patients' rights movement during the 1970s. In 1973 the American Hospital Association developed a patient's bill of rights. This document stated that health-care facilities were responsible for seeing that patients made informed decisions about their health care. As a result of this movement, physicians pledged to abide by a set of rules known as the doctrine of informed consent. They promised to *inform* patients exactly what their illness was, how they planned to treat it, and the risks, if any, involved. Armed with this knowledge, the patient could now *consent* to the medical treatment or refuse it.

The patients' rights movement also made demands about the right to die. Patients and their families objected to having doctors and states hold most of the power to make end-of-life decisions. They demanded more autonomy, and they took their demands to the courts.

These demands focused on two big issues. One was the right of a competent patient—or a surrogate acting for an incompetent patient—to

Cruzan v. Missouri and the Right to Die Debate

There are disabled people on both sides of the euthanasia debate. Shown here is Andrew Batavia, a lawyer who argued for physician-assisted suicide in front of the Supreme Court.

refuse life-support treatment. The other issue was physician-assisted suicide.

Support and Opposition

Like any movement, this one has opponents as well as supporters. Public opinion polls continue to show roughly as much opposition to right to die demands as support for them. In a 2000 poll, for instance, 1,477 people were asked, "If someone is terminally ill, is in great pain, and wants to kill themselves, should it be legal for a doctor to help them commit suicide, or not?" The results: 49 percent said yes, 45 percent said no, and 6 percent could not decide.[3]

The real decisions do not get made in public, though. They get made in courtrooms. That is where supporters and opponents square off. They present their cases to judges and justices, who make rulings that either pass new laws, agree with existing laws, amend them, or strike them down.

Later we will examine right to die laws, cases, and rulings. But first, let's take a look at key right to die issues through the eyes of supporters and opponents.

chapter 3
Through Supporters' Eyes

People who support the right to die and people who oppose it are both trying to deal with the issues, but the two sides disagree on what steps to take. They see the same facts from different points of view. Which point of view makes more sense? That will be for you to decide.

First we'll look at these issues through the eyes of right to die supporters. These supporters include some patients and their families and friends. They also include members of advocate groups who work on behalf of the right to choose to die.

In general, right to die supporters agree with the following:

◇ A person's life belongs, first and foremost, to

that person, and not to his or her state or nation. So people should be free to choose to die if they wish.

⋄ Yes, the state has a genuine interest in protecting the lives of its citizens, but this interest should be confined to providing a safe and secure homeland. The state should not feel responsible for an individual's personal life-and-death decisions. The state's laws should honor the individual's right to choose death.

Now, how do right to die supporters see the specific issues?

Issue: When, if ever, should a competent, terminally ill patient who is on life-support equipment be allowed to die?
Supporters agree that competent patients' end-of-life requests should be granted, and in fact they usually are. Most hospitals will honor these requests as long as they meet the doctrine of informed consent and as long as they are truly autonomous. The decision must not be heavily influenced by people close to the patient, such as family and friends.

Issue: When, if ever, should an incompetent patient in a persistent vegetative state be allowed to die?
Supporters point out that PVS patients are only technically alive. They are not aware of their

surroundings, and life without awareness is not really life. Since these patients have virtually no hope of regaining consciousness, they should be allowed to die a peaceful, natural death. The dying process should not be artificially prolonged by life-support technologies, such as respirators and feeding tubes. Here are their reasons why.

The psychological cost. Hooking up a PVS patient to these tubes and machines is an insult to the patient's dignity and puts the patient's family and friends through ongoing misery, supporters say.

The dollars-and-cents cost. Supporters point out that hospital resources are limited. Many PVS patients are cared for in intensive care units (ICUs). Health costs keep soaring, and ICUs are the most expensive units in a hospital. Physicians must carefully ration these beds. In 2002, ICU physicians were polled about their patients. Seventy-four percent said they would withhold ICU care from patients who would benefit little from it, such as PVS patients. Instead, they would favor caring for patients who stand some chance of getting better.[1] Supporters agree.

A doctor's duty. Some physicians' groups support the right to die. One of these groups filed an *amicus curiae* brief to the U.S. Supreme Court in the *Cruzan* case.

Through Supporters' Eyes

What Is an *Amicus Curiae* Brief?

This is an opinion filed with a court by an organization or individual who is highly interested in the case but is not directly involved. *Amicus curiae* means "friend of the court." The brief supports one side or the other. It has no legal authority, but it may help influence the court's final decision.

The group was the American Academy of Neurology (AAN), an organization of doctors who specialize in diseases of the brain and nervous system. In their brief, the AAN argued that a doctor should treat an unconscious patient only as long as the patient has a chance of getting better, which Nancy Cruzan did not have. According to the AAN, her medical treatment should cease and Nancy Cruzan should be allowed to die. Right to die supporters agreed.

Pain. Death cannot be painful for a PVS patient, since the patient is unconscious, supporters say. Unhooking a feeding and hydration tube will result in death within about two weeks. The unconscious patient will feel no pain of any kind.

Issue: **Who should be allowed to make end-of-life decisions?**

Supporters of the right to die believe that patients

themselves should make end-of-life medical decisions, not doctors or the state. Since PVS patients cannot speak for themselves, other people must make end-of-life decisions for them, under the doctrine of substituted judgment. Supporters believe these decisions should be based on what patients would wish if they could speak for themselves. But how can we know these wishes? Where will this information come from? Here are the sources.

Family and friends. Patients' family and friends are one source. In the past, patients may have told people close to them how they felt about end-of-life issues. Family and friends of Nancy Cruzan testified that several years before the accident, Nancy had told them that she would not want to go on living in a persistent vegetative state.

However, the courts did not find their testimony convincing. Another source of information about a patient's end-of-life wishes, an advance directive, would probably have been more convincing.

Advance directives. These are legal documents that patients wrote at an earlier time, when they were fully competent, signed by the patient and by witnesses. The patient keeps the original document in a safe place and gives copies to his or her doctor and to family members or friends. A typical advance directive states that, if the patient ever falls into PVS, life-support measures should not be used to keep him or her alive. An advance directive may also state the opposite—that life-support measures *should* be used to keep the patient alive.

Bioethics committees. Most big-city hospitals today have bioethics committees, which can be composed of nurses, lawyers, social workers, chaplains, philosophers, and citizen representatives. They make recommendations about end-of-life decisions in PVS cases where there is no advance directive. Many right to die supporters favor listening to what these committees recommend.

Issue: **When, if ever, should a physician help a patient die?**

Most right to die supporters favor physician-assisted suicide (PAS). In PAS, the doctor supplies the means, usually a lethal dose of drugs, to help the patient end his or her life.

But first, certain conditions must be met:

- ◇ The patient must be terminally ill.
- ◇ The patient must clearly understand the nature of his or her medical condition.
- ◇ The patient's decision must be autonomous. It cannot be made under pressure from family members or friends.
- ◇ This cannot be a snap decision. The patient must make the request several times over a period of weeks or months.

At the present time, Oregon is the only state where PAS is legal. Most right to die supporters would like to see PAS legalized in all fifty states. Here are their reasons why.

PAS is already a reality. Surveys show that some physicians help terminally ill patients to die.[2] They give these patients doses of a pain-killing drug, such as morphine, to reduce their discomfort. These physicians know that they may be giving these patients enough of the drug to cause death, but they are not directly causing their death.

This is known as the doctrine of double effect. The first effect, or purpose, is to reduce the patient's pain. The second effect is to bring about the patient's death. Doctors aim at the first effect, but know that the second may result. They believe it is the right and merciful thing to do. Supporters agree.

Physicians' roles have changed. It may seem shocking for physicians to take part in ending a human life. After all, a physician's traditional role is that of a healer. But in 1973, *Roe* v. *Wade* changed that role. Now doctors may legally perform abortions, ending an unborn child's life, when the pregnant woman requests it. Supporters argue that this new role should be expanded, and doctors should be allowed to take part in PAS when terminally ill patients request their help.

PAS offers relief from suffering. Peter Singer is a bioethicist who studies the risks and benefits of right to die treatments. He is well known for his support of the right to die. He writes, "The evidence shows that many people approaching the end of their lives fear suffering much more than death." Medication can ease their pain but not their fear of death. This, he writes, is why every terminally ill patient should have "the right to medical assistance in dying when this is in accordance with a person's persistent, informed, and autonomous request."[3]

PAS allows death with dignity. Supporters point out that many terminally ill patients do not wish to end their life in a helpless condition, hooked up to tubes and machines. They would rather die before the fatal disease runs its course.

Pierre Ludington, who tested positive for the AIDS virus, described what he would wish to do if he became debilitated, with no hope of recovery. First he would get a lethal dose of drugs from a physician. Then, he said, "I envision having a wonderful meal with friends. After they leave, I'll sit in front of the fire listening to Mozart, mix everything with brandy, sip it, and somebody will find me."[4]

PAS is not morally wrong. Many right to die

supporters see their lives as belonging, first and foremost, to themselves. If they believe in God, they do not see God as wanting them to suffer unnecessarily. As primary owners of their life, they see no moral problem with ending it when and as they see fit.

Issue: **Would legalizing PAS lead us down the "slippery slope"?**

When people urge caution, they sometimes use the slippery-slope argument. The basic idea behind this kind of argument is that if society takes the

Currently, Oregon is the only state that permits physician-assisted suicide. The state has been the site of legal and legislative battles over the issue.

first step in the wrong direction (down the slope), then it inevitably ends up with unintended negative consequences (at the bottom). Right to die opponents insist that legalizing PAS will lead us to legalize active euthanasia and mercy killing. How are these procedures different from PAS?

In PAS, once the drugs are supplied, the doctor's role ends. The patient must take the drugs alone, without the doctor's help. Elizabeth Bouvia, remember, would have needed more assistance. The doctor, or someone else, would have had to place the drugs in her mouth. To take this additional step is to commit active euthanasia.

Mercy killing is a step beyond this. This term is sometimes used to refer to the killing of severely handicapped infants or of incompetent adults who are suffering but have not asked for death. In either case, the person is killed painlessly. Neither mercy killing nor active euthanasia is legal in any of the fifty states.

But what if these measures do become legal? In 1989 the U.S. Civil Rights Commission issued a report that strongly criticized allowing severely handicapped infants to die.[5] Right to die opponents agree. They argue that going down this slippery slope will lead us to kill more and more sick, elderly, and handicapped people who want to live, not die. These innocent human beings will be killed because they are a physical and financial burden on the people who must care for them, opponents say.

Right to die supporters call this slippery-slope argument emotional, illogical, and unrealistic. Don't doctors know the difference between helping terminally ill people who wish to die and murdering people who want to live? Of course they do, supporters say. They claim that forcing doctors to ignore the pleas of terminal patients who wish to die is far more likely to make doctors insensitive to human suffering than legalizing PAS.

In short, supporters say, the right to die is a freedom that belongs in a democracy like the United States of America, where the legal powers of the state are limited and personal autonomy is honored.

chapter 4

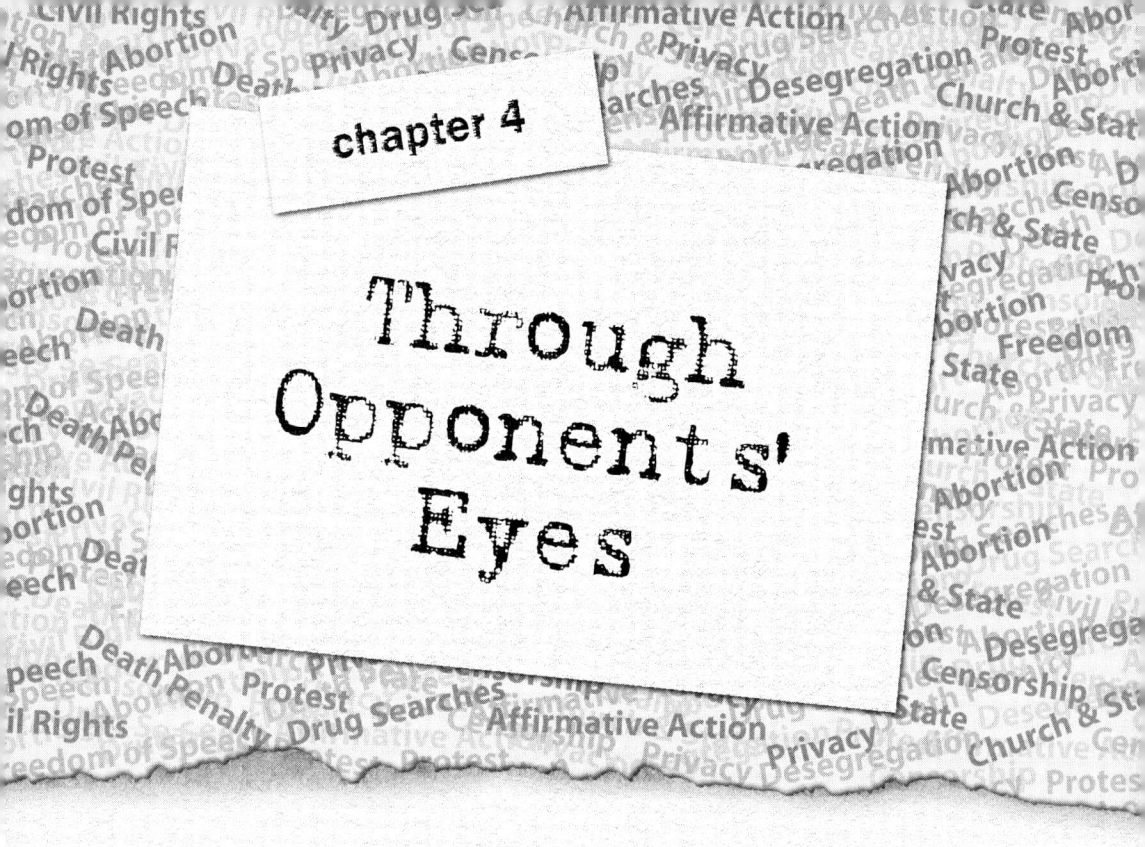

Through Opponents' Eyes

Right to die opponents include right-to-life groups, disability-rights groups, and many branches of organized religions.

In general, right to die opponents agree with the following:

- ◇ A person should live his or her life through to the very end. Religious opponents believe that life is sacred and that only God should determine when a person will die.

- ◇ It is the state's responsibility to protect and preserve human life. It is a physician's responsibility to cure and comfort patients, not help them to die.

Now, how do opponents of the right to die see the issues involved?

Issue: **When, if ever, should a competent, terminally ill patient on life-support equipment be allowed to die?**

Some right to die opponents agree with right to die supporters on this issue. They feel that requests to withhold or terminate care should be granted. The way they see it, the patient's time to die has already come, and life-support measures are only interfering with a natural death.

In 2003, the Catholic Bishops of Florida addressed this issue. Their statement says that withholding extraordinary life-support measures from terminally ill patients "may be seen as an expression of our hope in the life to come."[1] This reminds us of people's attitudes toward death and dying one hundred years ago, when they were more likely to accept it and less likely to fight it.

Other, hard-line right to die opponents hold fast to their stand that physicians and other health-care providers must never help end a patient's life under any circumstances—even when all that means is withholding extraordinary care. They believe everything must be done to save a person's life, no matter how ill the person is.

Issue: **When, if ever, should an incompetent patient in a persistent vegetative state be allowed to die?**

Opponents are also split on this issue. Some say never. Others say sometimes. Let's see why.

Through Opponents' Eyes

Those who say never. Hard-line opponents emphasize that PVS patients are living human beings. While they may not be technically conscious, they still can do some of the things that fully conscious people do. Many can breathe on their own. They go through alternating periods of sleep and wakefulness. During wakefulness, their eyes can sometimes follow moving objects. They may cry out or twitch when they hear a sudden noise.

Hard-line opponents also point out that PVS patients are not terminally ill (according to the definition of having less than six months to live). Some can go on living indefinitely. True, they probably never will recover. But prospects for recovery should not dictate whether they live or die.

Christian right-to-life groups take this stand. So do some physicians' groups, including the Association of American Physicians and Surgeons. Like the American Academy of Neurology (AAN), this physicians' group also submitted an *amicus curiae* brief to the U.S. Supreme Court in the *Cruzan* case.

But while the AAN firmly supported Nancy Cruzan's right to choose to die, the Association of American Physicians and Surgeons firmly opposed it. In its brief, the organization wrote,

> The obligation of the physician to the comatose, vegetative, or developmentally disabled patient

does not depend upon the prospect for recovery. The physician must always act on behalf of the patient's well-being.[2]

Those who say sometimes. In this country, the Roman Catholic Church has traditionally been a hard-line opponent in all right to die issues. But their opposition has softened when it comes to withholding life-support measures for terminally ill and PVS patients.

In 1980 the Church issued a declaration in favor of "the right to die peacefully with human and Christian dignity." It stated that "the use of therapeutic means can sometimes pose problems" and that it is "permissible to make do with the normal means that medicine can offer." The declaration went on to state that refusing extraordinary life support "is not the equivalent of suicide; on the contrary, it should be considered as an acceptance of the human condition . . . or a desire not to impose excessive expense on the family or the community."[3]

The declaration was not specific about which life-support measures could be withheld. Most Church officials agreed that respirators could be withheld but not feeding and hydration tubes, since giving patients food and water amounts to normal care, even if the means of giving it are extraordinary.

Feeding tubes were originally intended not for

terminally ill patients but for people recovering from injury or surgery that made it difficult to eat on their own. For these patients, feeding tubes were a temporary measure. Later on, they became part of the extraordinary medical technology used to keep PVS patients alive indefinitely. In addition, people have pointed out that many dying people stop eating as part of the body's shutting down—and feeding tubes interfere with this natural part of the dying process.[4]

Since 1980, some Church officials have changed their opinion on tube feeding. In 1994, the Reverend William G. Most wrote that food could be withheld from PVS patients if the "difficulty, expense, and care of providing it" are too great.[5]

Issue: **Who should be allowed to make end-of-life decisions?**

Right to die opponents are split on this issue as well. Some agree that family members and friends should make end-of-life decisions for incompetent patients. Catholic bishop Robert N. Lynch writes,

> When a person is not competent to make his or her own decisions, it is very appropriate for a family member or guardian to be designated . . . to represent the patient's interests and interpret his or her wishes.[6]

Bishop Lynch also writes, "It is extremely important for all to have designated a medical proxy to someone who is trusted and to leave a 'living will' in which you indicate your wishes."[7]

A living will is an advance directive in which you state whether you wish to receive life-prolonging medical treatment if you become ill with no hope of recovery and are not competent to communicate your wishes directly. Most living wills ask that respirators, feeding tubes, and other life-prolonging equipment be withheld so that the patient may die a natural death.

A medical, or health-care, proxy gives an extra step of protection. It is another type of advance directive. It names someone to interpret your living will for doctors in case there is any confusion about your wishes. It is sometimes called a durable health-care power of attorney.

Other right to die opponents disagree with Bishop Lynch about allowing family and friends to make end-of-life decisions for incompetent patients. They are suspicious of allowing anyone to make these decisions. They worry about outside pressures from family and friends who, for their own selfish reasons, might want the patient to die. Mary Senander is president of Human Life Alliance, a right-to-life advocate group based in Minnesota. She says, "The unspoken purpose of the Living Will is to hasten or encourage death, directly or indirectly."[8] The Ohio Right to Life advocate group calls living wills "unnecessary and dangerous for patients, doctors and society."[9]

Issue: **When, if ever, should a physician help a patient die?**

On this issue there is no disagreement. Right to die opponents firmly oppose physician-assisted suicide. Here are their reasons why.

PAS violates a physician's foremost duty. "I will give no deadly medicine to any one if asked, nor suggest any such counsel. . . ."[10] These are the words of Hippocrates, an ancient Greek physician. They come from the Hippocratic Oath, a pledge that many medical school students still make today, in an amended version, as they prepare to begin practical training as doctors.

The oath shows that PAS is not a new issue. At the time Hippocrates wrote it, in 400 B.C., PAS was a common practice in ancient Greek society. Hippocrates was on the minority side in the debate over PAS.

Opponents say that this ancient pledge still defines a physician's foremost duties: to heal patients and never to harm them. Tom Horkan, executive director of the Florida Catholic Conference, opposes the right to choose to die. He writes, "Up until now the medical profession has been about healing people. If it starts being about killing people, it's going to be a very dangerous thing."[11] The American Medical Association (AMA) is a professional society for physicians and patients nationwide. In its code of ethics, the AMA takes a strong position against PAS:

> Allowing physicians to participate in assisted suicide would cause more harm than good. . . . Instead of participating in assisted suicide, physicians must aggressively respond to the needs of patients at the end of life. Patients should not be abandoned once it is determined that cure is impossible.[12]

Legalizing PAS would undermine trust. Opponents warn that legalizing PAS would make some patients lose their trust in doctors. Very sick patients are often confused and anxious. Just knowing that people in the same hospital were dying with a doctor's help could terrify them. George Annas of Boston University's Schools of Medicine and Public Health speaks and writes about right to die issues. He warns, "A patient could never be totally confident that the doctor was coming to help him and not kill him."[13]

With PAS, there is no turning back. Suppose the patient does not *really* want to die? Most terminally ill patients who ask for PAS are actually crying out for help, opponents say. Studies show that most patients who ask for PAS are not in severe physical pain. Instead, they suffer from depression. They see themselves as a burden to others. But depression is treatable, not fatal. These patients need compassionate counseling from doctors, not lethal drugs, opponents say.

And what if the patient's diagnosis later proves incorrect? Opponents point to the case of Sidney Cohen. When physicians told him that cancer would kill him in less than three months, he fell into a deep depression and wished he were dead. He was in great pain and said he felt desperate and frightened.

But eight months later he was still alive. In the meantime, he had gotten improved treatment for pain. He still had cancer, but now, he said, "I feel that I'm living a full life, worth living."[14]

PAS is morally wrong. The Catholic Church and right-to-life groups oppose PAS on the same moral grounds that they oppose abortion. In its 1980 declaration, the Catholic Church stated,

> Nothing and no one can in any way permit the killing of an innocent human being, whether a fetus or an embryo, an infant or an adult, an old person, or one suffering from an incurable disease, or a person who is dying. . . . [PAS is a] violation of the divine law, an offense against the dignity of the human person, a crime against life, and an attack on humanity.[15]

Most world religions, including Islam, Hinduism, and Orthodox Judaism, condemn PAS on moral grounds. Some Protestant churches, such as the Episcopalian and the Unitarian

Universalist, do not strictly condemn PAS, but they do not recommend it either. Some denominations say that it is up to the individual to decide for himself or herself whether PAS is moral.

Members of right-to-life advocate groups are also outspoken PAS opponents. Hawaii Right to Life, for example, is "unequivocally opposed to the legalization of assisted suicide," primarily on moral grounds.[16]

Hospice makes PAS unnecessary. Hospice is a program for terminally ill patients that serves as an alternative to hospitals. The goal of hospice is to help terminally ill patients live out their last days comfortably, free of life-support equipment. There are some hospice facilities where patients are treated. But most hospice workers go directly to patients' homes and give them palliative medication, narcotics to control pain. Some hospice leaders argue that PAS is unnecessary, now that they have found ways to successfully manage pain and give comfort to the dying. Surveys show that both nurses and physicians in hospitals are not well trained in treating pain, while hospice workers are.[17]

Issue: **Would legalizing PAS lead us down the slippery slope?**

Right to die opponents believe that legalizing physician-assisted suicide would lead us down the slippery slope toward killing innocent people who have no wish to die. Father Matthew Habiger, president of Human Life International, a pro-life advocate group, puts it this way:

> The march toward a complete antilife philosophy can now be easily mapped: from contraception to abortion to euthanasia. Once life is no longer treated as a sacred gift from God, a society inevitably embraces death in all its forms.[18]

Why are opponents so certain that legalizing PAS will lead us down this slippery slope? Here are their reasons.

It has happened before. Supporters of PAS may have good intentions, opponents say, but so did President Theodore Roosevelt and U.S. Supreme Court justice Oliver Wendell Holmes when they supported the eugenics movement in the early part of the last century.

Eugenics means improving the human race by selective breeding. The idea was for the healthiest, most intelligent people to have many children and for the least healthy and least intelligent—the "unfit"—to have fewer (or none). As a result, the human race would become more healthy and intelligent.

These good intentions led to terrible consequences. Instead of just discouraging the "unfit" from breeding, state governments took direct physical action. States passed laws making it legal for people seen as "unfit" to be taken into custody and sterilized. In the United States, more than one hundred thousand people were sterilized against their will before the eugenics movement drew to an end in the 1930s.[19] In some states, though, sterilizing "unfit" people against their will remained legal until the 1970s.

Right to die opponents see eugenics as nothing but discrimination against people with physical and mental handicaps—and they view PAS the same way. They foresee a time in the not-too-distant future when the most vulnerable among us might again become victims if right to die supporters get their way.

It is happening now. In the European nation of the Netherlands, PAS and other forms of euthanasia are permitted. Euthanasia is not officially legal in the Netherlands, but it is not punished either, as long as it is performed according to government guidelines. Opponents point to the Remmelink report, a study of euthanasia in the Netherlands. According to this study, approximately thirty-five hundred cases of PAS and euthanasia are reported in a given year. In about one thousand of these cases, patients who were not competent were killed. These included newborn babies who had severe handicaps but were not dying. They were killed at the request of their parents.[20] Right to die opponents see the

Netherlands study as an example of the slippery slope in action. What is happening there could happen here, they insist, if PAS were legalized in the United States.

Infants, the elderly, and the disabled are particularly vulnerable. In 1982 a child with severe handicaps was born in an Indiana hospital. The child needed an operation, and his chances of surviving it were estimated to be less than 50 percent. In the meantime, the child would have to be tube fed.

The parents said no to the operation and no to tube feeding. They decided to let their child die instead. The hospital refused to honor the parents' decision and took them to court. To guard the family's identity, the courts called the child Infant Doe. A lower court and the Indiana Supreme Court both upheld the parents' decision, and Infant Doe was allowed to die.[21]

Nationwide, opponents of the right to die were outraged by the Indiana courts' decisions. They called the Infant Doe case a miscarriage of justice, a homicide, and a step down the slippery slope toward eugenics. In 1989 the U.S. Civil Rights Commission sided with right to die opponents in their report titled "Medical Discrimination Against Children with Disabilities." After looking at the Infant Doe case and others like it, the commission wrote that it "rejects the view that an acceptable

Cruzan v. Missouri *and the Right to Die Debate*

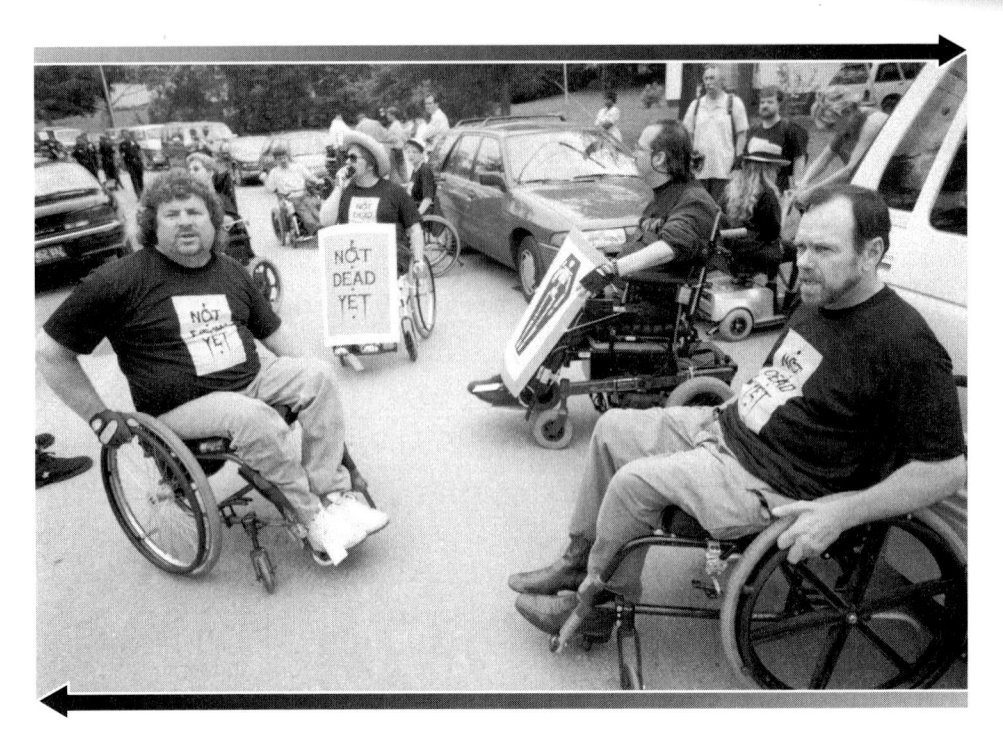

Some people argue that the sick, elderly, and disabled may be at risk if euthanasia is accepted by society. The group Not Dead Yet demonstrates here against physician-assisted suicide.

answer to discrimination and prejudice is to assure the 'right to die' to those against whom the discrimination and prejudice exists."[22]

Opponents of the right to die believe that elderly patients may be victimized, too. These patients could be pressured by family members into asking for physician-assisted suicide. In 1997, the editors of *The Nation*, a magazine about politics and legal issues, wrote:

> Very ill people may be vulnerable to suggestions from family members that they could make

everyone's life easier by ending their own. . . . Who could blame a wife, herself elderly and in poor health, for suggesting suicide to her terminally ill husband? But how free would his choice then be?[23]

Some disability-rights groups also see PAS and the right to die as excuses for discrimination. One of these groups, Not Dead Yet, writes, "people with disabilities do not see much evidence that the courts treat their lives as being as valuable as their nondisabled counterparts."[24]

In short, opponents feel this way: The more laws supporting the right to die that legislators pass, the closer society comes to devaluing life for more and more people. Supporters, on the other hand, feel that the more laws supporting the right to die we pass, the freer a people we become. The next chapter takes a close look at these laws.

chapter 5

Right to Die Laws

The laws that legislatures, justices, and judges make are neither absolute nor unchanging. As we know, human beings must constantly put new laws on the books and remake old ones to reflect the shifting concerns of human society.

These laws are meant to be balanced, to be fair and just, reflecting the concerns of all citizens. With a matter as controversial as the right to die, achieving this balance is an ongoing struggle. Let's take a look at lawmakers' struggles to deal with the conflicting concerns of right to die supporters and opponents.

Common Law

We'll start by defining the three kinds of laws involved. First, there's common law. This is a collection of principles based on the laws of England and the American colonies before the American Revolution. These principles are not actually on the books now, but people have been following them for hundreds of years.

U.S. courts have always recognized common law as the basis for existing laws. The U.S. Supreme Court used common law in its 1891 *Botsford* ruling. The Court found that the right to refuse medical treatment is based on the common-law right "of every individual to the possession and control of his own person, free from all restraint or interference of others. . . ."[1]

This same common-law principle is the basis for the right of competent terminally ill adults to refuse extraordinary medical treatment, such as respirators and feeding tubes, even when this refusal will hasten their death.

State and Federal Laws

State laws apply only to people within that state. Federal laws apply to everyone in all fifty states. When the U.S. Supreme Court legalized abortion in *Roe v. Wade* (1973), it made a federal law. *Roe* made abortion legal in all fifty states. Individual states could still make their own laws about abortion. For example, the states of Idaho, Kentucky, Missouri, North Dakota, and Rhode Island prohibit insurance coverage for abortion unless the patient has paid a special premium. But they could not make abortion illegal.

By contrast, in its ruling on *Cruzan* v. *Missouri* (1990), the Court made no federal law. The ruling applied only to that particular case. At present there are no federal laws legalizing or prohibiting the right to choose to die.

There are state laws, though—lots of them. In its 1997 ruling in *Washington* v. *Glucksberg*, the U.S. Supreme Court assured the states that they had the right to pass their own laws about physician-assisted suicide. States may make rulings on other right to die issues as well, including advance directives.

Advance Directives

The first state to pass a law about making living wills was California, in 1976. Ten more states followed the same year. But not all states joined them. In her *Cruzan* opinion in 1990, U.S. Supreme Court justice Sandra Day O'Connor urged all states to pass laws allowing living wills and health-care proxies. Today, all fifty states have these kinds of laws on the books.

But these state laws present serious problems. For one thing, they vary from state to state, and many doctors and hospitals will honor advance directives only in the state in which the patient lives. To be truly safe, people would have to execute living wills in every single state they might ever visit.

Right to Die Laws

In addition, some state laws have tricky legal loopholes. Estelle Browning fell victim to one of these loopholes. In 1985, she wrote a living will in Florida, stating that if she ever fell into a persistent vegetative state, doctors should withhold life-support equipment and allow her to die. Then a massive stroke in 1986 left her in PVS.

According to her living will, Browning should have been allowed to die. But when she wrote it, she did not know that living wills in Florida were valid only for terminally ill patients. Living wills did not work for PVS patients like her, who were not terminally ill.

So Estelle Browning had to live on. She died in 1989, still in a persistent vegetative state. The Estelle Browning case got lots of media attention. As a result, a year later, the Florida Supreme Court closed the loophole by extending the living-will option to patients who are not terminally ill.

Knowing the Score

Advance directives will not help people who do not take advantage of them. Surveys show that few people have advance directives, and many people do not even know what they are. Surveys also show that hospitals, nursing homes, and other health-care institutions do not always pay attention to advance directives.[2]

To combat these problems, federal lawmakers

passed the Patient Self-Determination Act (PSDA), which became effective in 1991. The PSDA requires public health-care institutions to honor advance directives. If an institution does not, it can lose federal Medicare and Medicaid funding, which make up a big share of its income.

PSDA benefits health-care workers as well as patients. Surveys show that many physicians, nurses, and health-care administrators do not know enough about advance directives.[3] PSDA forces them to write up their own policies about terminating life-support treatment and share those policies with patients. Then everyone on both sides will know the score.

These policies also include information on Do Not Resuscitate orders. Nancy Cruzan was resuscitated by emergency medical technicians (EMTs) at the scene of her accident. Her breathing and heartbeat had stopped, so the EMTs gave her cardiopulmonary resuscitation (CPR), which involves alternately breathing into the patient's mouth to get the lungs working and pushing in on the rib cage to revive the heart.

The EMTs succeeded, but not before Nancy's brain had suffered irreversible catastrophic harm. A Do Not Resuscitate order (DNR) tells medical professionals that this person does not want them to perform CPR if his or her breathing and heartbeat have stopped. DNRs are usually taken out by terminally ill patients. People with DNRs are advised to have copies of the order with them at all times, in their wallets, purses, and automobile glove compartments.

Dead or Alive?

By the time the EMTs revived Nancy Cruzan, her higher brain functions had ceased. She was no longer conscious, and never would be again. But Nancy was not legally dead. Her higher brain functions were gone forever, but her whole brain was not dead. A small part, the brain stem, was still operating. That is why her lungs could still breathe and her heart could still beat.

As right to die opponents point out, miracles do happen. A very few people have regained consciousness after decades of existing in a state of unconsciousness—but not a persistent vegetative state. There are no documented cases of a person's full recovery from PVS.

Still, state laws take a cautious route when it comes to defining death. For now, whole-brain death remains the official legal standard in all fifty states.

PAS and the Law

Physician-assisted suicide is a crime in most places in the world. Switzerland, Belgium, and the Netherlands are the only nations where PAS is truly legal.[4]

Cruzan v. Missouri and the Right to Die Debate

What about the United States? In its 1997 *Washington* v. *Glucksberg* decision, the U.S. Supreme Court ruled that the Constitution does not guarantee people the right to commit suicide with a doctor's assistance. But the Court did not make PAS a federal crime. Each state must make its own laws about PAS.

Normally, elected lawmakers are the people who propose and vote on state laws. But in some states, private citizens may also do this. In 1994, Oregon Death With Dignity, a right to die advocate group, spearheaded a proposal to legalize PAS in Oregon. This proposal was called Measure 16. Under this proposal, terminally ill patients in Oregon could obtain a lethal dose of drugs if two doctors certified that the patient's request met the doctrine of informed consent.

In November 1994, Oregon voters passed Measure 16 by a narrow margin, 52 percent to 48 percent. Right to die opponents then launched a long legal battle. Finally, supporters won in the courts. In 1997, Measure 16 went into effect. Opponents tried to repeal Measure 16 in a state referendum, but were unsuccessful.

At present, only Oregon has legalized PAS. Meanwhile, thirty-five other states have made it illegal, while the remaining fourteen have stayed neutral. But wherever it occurs, PAS is rarely punished. Surveys show that one in five doctors and

Right to Die Laws

one in five nurses have helped terminally ill patients commit suicide. Yet in a forty-year stretch, from 1950 to 1993, only eleven doctors in the United States were prosecuted for PAS, and almost none went to prison.[5]

Dr. Death

One man is a notorious exception to this rule. He is Dr. Jack Kevorkian, also known as Dr. Death. Kevorkian began performing assisted suicide on a regular basis in 1990. He used what he called his Mercitron machine: three bottles containing drugs hung from a wood frame. A single tube connecting the three bottles ran into a syringe, which Kevorkian would insert into the patient's arm. The patient would then push the plunger in, injecting the lethal mixture. Seconds later the patient would be unconscious, and minutes later, the patient would be dead.

During the 1990s Kevorkian assisted in some 130 suicides of terminally ill patients and nonterminal patients with degenerative diseases such as Alzheimer's and cystic fibrosis. He worked in private, often in the patient's home.

Doctors who assist patients to die can be reasonably sure that the law will ignore them, provided they work quietly. But Kevorkian very much wanted people to know what he was doing. He had a cause. He needed to persuade voters and

59

lawmakers to legalize PAS. In a 1993 *ABC News* interview, he said, "When society reaches the age of enlightenment, then they'll call me and other doctors Dr. Life."[6]

To Permit or to Punish?

The state of Michigan took away Dr. Kevorkian's medical license, but he kept assisting patients to die. The doctor stood trial in Michigan courts four different times without being convicted. Judges and juries remained reluctant to penalize a physician for PAS, even a physician without a legal license to practice.

Finally, though, Kevorkian went a step too far. He videotaped a death and had the tape shown on the CBS television program *60 Minutes*. The patient, Thomas Youk, age fifty-two, suffered from a terminal illness, amyotrophic lateral sclerosis, or ALS. This nerve disease—also called Lou Gehrig's disease—eventually causes complete paralysis. Youk was not able to administer the drugs himself.

On the tape, Kevorkian himself is seen actively giving Thomas Youk the lethal injection. Kevorkian had gone a step beyond PAS. He had committed active euthanasia. In the eyes of the law, he had committed murder.

Dr. Jack Kevorkian was tried and convicted of second-degree murder in a Michigan court. In

Right to Die Laws

Dr. Jack Kevorkian, an outspoken supporter of euthanasia, is shown here during his 1999 trial in Michigan.

April 1999 he was sentenced to ten to twenty-five years in prison. Judge Jessica Cooper told him, "You had the audacity to go on national television, show the world what you did and dare the legal system to stop you. Well, sir, consider yourself stopped."[7]

chapter 6

Lower Court Cases

Laws concerning the right to choose to die are not always enforced, as we have seen. Sometimes juries and judges look the other way. But when these laws are enforced, as they were with Jack Kevorkian, they can lead to serious consequences. Let's take a close look at how courts make rulings in right to die cases.

We know that courts base their rulings on the facts of the case and the laws that apply. But judges and juries also look at past rulings for guidance. Every ruling has the potential to set precedent. (Precedents are past cases that lawyers and judges look back on and cite, or mention, to help them argue and rule on the cases they are working on.)

Cruzan v. Missouri *and the Right to Die Debate*

In this chapter we'll look at precedent-setting lower court rulings in right to die cases. Then, in chapter 7, we'll see how these lower-court rulings influenced the U.S. Supreme Court decision in *Cruzan* v. *Missouri*.

The Facts of the Case

The first and most influential lower court right to die case of all is *In re Quinlan*. This landmark case was tried in the Supreme Court of New Jersey, the highest court in that state, in 1976. As you review this case, notice the similarities to the case of Nancy Cruzan.

In April 1975, Karen Ann Quinlan was twenty-one years old. Suddenly one evening she stopped breathing. Why this happened is not entirely clear. Karen shared a house in Cranberry Lake, New Jersey. Her housemates said she was drinking liquor that night and had taken a Valium, a tranquilizer drug. These substances together may have played a part in the tragedy.

At first her housemates thought Karen had fallen asleep, and they left her alone. Then they noticed that her skin had turned bluish-gray and cold. By the time an EMT crew arrived, Karen's brain had been without oxygen for a half hour or so.

The EMTs managed to get her lungs breathing and heart beating. Her skin turned pink again, but she could not breathe on her own. In the intensive care unit of Newton Memorial Hospital, physicians hooked Karen up to a respirator. As time passed, doctors saw that her brain stem was still working, but that her higher-brain activities had ceased. She had fallen into a persistent vegetative state.

A Different Person

Karen was transferred to St. Clare's, a Catholic hospital with more advanced life-support equipment. Now, in addition to a respirator, she was hooked up to four tubes that pumped fluids into her body. Imagine seeing the daughter you love lying on a hospital bed. She is right there in front of you, but she is not fully there. Her body is present, but her mind is absent. One July evening, looking down at his daughter, Joseph Quinlan thought, "Karen is never going to be alive again as I have known her. I have to accept that."[1]

So Karen's parents instructed her physician, Robert Morse, to unhook her from all life-support devices and allow her to die a natural death.

This put Dr. Morse in a serious dilemma. Karen's brain stem was still alive, so according to New Jersey law, Karen herself was still alive. If Dr. Morse took Karen off life support, he could be charged with murder.

This left the Quinlans in a dilemma of their own. They believed that if Karen could be made aware of her hopeless state, she would wish to die a natural death. They felt it was their duty to grant Karen this final wish. So they hired a lawyer and took the matter to court.

The Arguments

A trial court headed by Judge Robert Muir heard the arguments. Karen's mother testified that, years earlier, she and Karen had discussed life-and-death matters, and Karen said that she would never want to be kept alive if she were in PVS. This was her wish. Karen's friends gave similar testimony.

The Quinlans' lawyer argued that based on this testimony, Karen's parents should be allowed to act as surrogates, or substitutes, for Karen and carry out her wishes, under the doctrine of substituted judgment. Karen's wish, the attorney argued, should override the state's interest in protecting her life.

Dr. Morse's attorney strongly disagreed. He argued that Karen's death would start us moving down the slippery slope toward eugenics, exterminating more and more incompetent victims. These victims would include the severely physically disabled, the senile, and the mentally retarded. It was the state's right and responsibility to preserve not only Karen Ann Quinlan's life, he said, but the lives of all Americans.

In March 1976, Judge Muir ruled in favor of Dr. Morse. The judge based his decision largely on the state's right and responsibility to preserve and protect human life. He discounted testimony about Karen's wish to be taken off life support, since she was healthy and not facing death when she made it. Removing Karen from life support, he ruled, would be an act of homicide.

The Final Ruling

The Quinlans appealed Judge Muir's ruling to the New Jersey Supreme Court. Each side presented roughly the same arguments as they had at the first trial, but this time to a panel of justices. On March 31, 1976, the New Jersey Supreme Court justices announced their decision in the appeals case of *In re Quinlan*.

Sometimes rulings depend upon point of view. Judge Muir of the trial court wrote his ruling largely from the state's point of view. The New Jersey Supreme Court justices, on the other hand, tried to put themselves in Karen Ann Quinlan's shoes. What would she want?

Based on the testimony of Karen's parents and friends, the justices concluded,

> If Karen were herself miraculously lucid for an interval . . . and perceptive of her irreversible condition, she could effectively decide upon discontinuance of the life-support apparatus, even if it meant the prospect of natural death.[2]

So, the justices decided, Karen would wish to refuse life support and die a natural death. But did her parents have the right to make this decision for her?

Judge Muir had ruled that they did not. The justices disagreed. There are times when an individual's constitutionally protected right to privacy overrules the state's interest in protecting life, they said. In order to guard Karen's right of privacy, her family should be allowed to decide for her.

Judge Muir also had ruled that detaching Karen from life-support equipment would be an act of murder. Again, the justices disagreed. They ruled that if the Quinlans chose to have Karen detached from the respirator, the doctor who did this would not be committing a crime.

Soon after the ruling, the respirator was unhooked. But Karen went on breathing on her

In re Quinlan (1976) set precedents for

◇ supporting a patient's right to privacy, including the power to refuse unwanted medical treatment;

◇ supporting the power of a surrogate to assert this right for an incompetent patient under the doctrine of substituted judgment.

own. Karen's parents would not allow the feeding tube to be removed, though, and Karen lived on for several years in PVS until she died in 1985.

More Precedents

The *Quinlan* case was the first right to die case that received national media attention. It was destined to influence similar cases for years to come.

Now let's look at four other lower court cases that set precedents of their own. As you review each one, keep in mind that it will influence the U.S. Supreme Court ruling in the most important right to die case of all, *Cruzan* v. *Missouri* (1990), discussed in chapter 7.

Superintendent of Belchertown State School v. **Saikewicz**, *Supreme Judicial Court of Massachusetts (1977).* Joseph Saikewicz was a sixty-seven-year-old man with the mental abilities of a child of two years eight months. He suffered from terminal cancer, which could be treated with chemotherapy. Saikewicz's guardian was against this treatment. He said it would cause the patient great pain and would lengthen his life by only a few months. The state objected, citing its responsibility for protecting life.

As in *Quinlan*, the justices sided with the guardian. But the *Saikewicz* ruling contained an important difference from *Quinlan*. The justices

Saikewicz (1977) set a precedent for

◇ supporting an incompetent terminally ill patient's right to privacy, including the power to refuse unwanted medical treatment;

◇ but only if decided by the court.

ruled that the decision should not be made by friends and family but by the court itself.

***In re Storar**, Court of Appeals of New York (1981)*. This precedent-setting case is really two cases decided together. The first concerns John Storar, age fifty-two, a severely retarded man with terminal cancer. A state official wanted Mr. Storar to receive blood transfusions to prolong his life. His guardian, his mother, did not. The transfusions would cause him pain and prolong his life only a short time, she said.

The second case concerns Brother Joseph Charles Fox, age eighty-three, a member of the Society of Mary, who was in PVS. A respirator kept him alive. His guardian, Father Philip K. Eichner, wanted the respirator removed. While Fox was still competent, Eichner testified, Fox had told him that this would be his wish.

In the *Storar* case, the court ruled against the

Lower Court Cases

***In re Storar* (1981) set a precedent for**

⬥ supporting a surrogate's power to refuse unwanted medical treatment for an incompetent patient;

⬥ but only if there is clear and convincing evidence of the patient's wishes while competent.

guardian, since the patient, who was born severely retarded, had never been able to express his wishes. In the Fox case, the court sided with the guardian, since the patient had made his wishes known while still competent.

Both decisions hinged on clear and convincing evidence. In the case of Fox, that evidence was present. In the case of Storar, it was not.

***In re Conroy**, Supreme Court of New Jersey (1985)*. Claire Conroy, age eighty-four, suffered from Alzheimer's disease and other serious and irreversible conditions. Physicians at her nursing home had installed a feeding tube. Her guardian, her nephew, wanted the tube removed to allow her to die. Ms. Conroy's doctors refused.

The New Jersey justices sided with the doctors, and Claire Conroy was not allowed to die. If there had been clear and convincing evidence of the incompetent patient's wish to forgo medical treatment under these circumstances, and if the patient's suffering clearly outweighed the benefits of living, the justices might have sided with the guardian. However, they wrote, clear and convincing evidence is not *always* necessary. If the burdens of the patient's life with the treatment clearly outweigh the benefits the patient gets from life, the patient may be allowed to die. So, though *Conroy* favored the doctors, it still set a strong precedent in favor of the right to choose to die.

***In re Westchester County Medical Center on behalf of O'Connor**, Court of Appeals of New York (1988).* The circumstances here are similar to those of *In re Conroy*. The patient in the case was a seventy-seven-year-old woman who became incompetent after a series of strokes. The hospital wanted to insert a feeding tube, but family members objected. They testified that years earlier the patient had told them that she would not want to be kept alive under these circumstances.

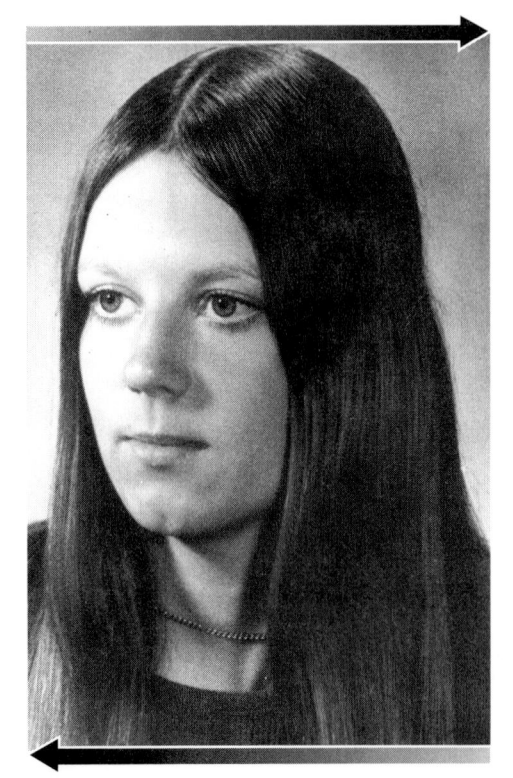

Karen Ann Quinlan, who went into PVS when she was twenty-two. Her family's legal fight to get her respirator turned off gained national attention for the right to die debate.

In re Conroy (1985) set a precedent for

◇ supporting a surrogate's power to refuse unwanted medical treatment for an incompetent patient without clear and convincing evidence of the patient's wishes;

◇ including the removal of feeding tubes;

◇ provided the patient's suffering clearly outweighs the benefits of treatment.

The New York appeals court justices sided with the hospital. The justices decided that the family members' testimony did not present clear and convincing evidence of the patient's wishes.

In their ruling, the New York justices disagreed with the *Conroy* ruling on two major points. First, the New York justices ruled that without clear and convincing evidence of the patient's wishes, medical treatment could not be withheld. Second, they ruled that without this evidence, no one could decide whether an incompetent patient's life was still worth living.

Reaction

The *Quinlan* and *Conroy* rulings drew especially strong reactions. Much of the reaction to *In re Quinlan* was positive. From coast to coast, people expressed their support. An editorial in the

Chicago Tribune newspaper stated, "Millions of us supported the Quinlans' courageous determination to give their daughter the right to die when the right to life had lost all meaning."[3]

Much of the reaction to *In re Conroy* was negative. Right to die opponents called it a move toward legalizing mercy killing and a step down the slippery slope toward eugenics. The president of the National Right to Life Committee said the decision changed "all rules which protected your life and mine."[4]

We can see both agreement and disagreement when we review these five lower court cases (*Quinlan, Saikewicz, Storar, Conroy,* and *O'Connor*). The lower courts agree on the

O'Connor (1988) set a precedent for

- supporting a patient's right to privacy, including the power to refuse unwanted medical treatment, including the removal of feeding tubes;
- but not through a surrogate unless clear and convincing evidence of the patient's wishes are presented;
- and not because the surrogate or the court feels that the patient's suffering outweighs the benefits of the treatment.

Lower Court Cases

fundamental, common-law right of a patient to refuse medical treatment. And the courts are willing to accept the right of a surrogate, under certain conditions, to refuse treatment on behalf of an incompetent patient. But beyond these two points, we see a great deal of disagreement—which is just what U.S. Supreme Court justices saw when they took on their first right to die case.

chapter 7

U.S. Supreme Court Cases

Most cases come to the U.S. Supreme Court from the lower courts on appeal. The Court turns down far more of these appeals than it accepts. The nine justices take on only those cases that they feel are the most important ones. Often they accept an appeal because it deals with issues they have never ruled on before. The Court accepted its first right to die case in 1989.

Cruzan v. *Missouri* became a historic U.S. Supreme Court case and a nationwide issue. Even before the case was decided, newspapers, magazines, television news shows, politicians, physicians' groups, and philosophers published their opinions. Feelings were very strong on both sides of the issue.

The *Cruzan* case came to the U.S. Supreme Court on appeal from a ruling made by the Supreme Court of Missouri in the case of *Cruzan* v. *Harmon*. Let's look at that lower court ruling first.

The Facts of the Case

In 1983, twenty-five-year-old Nancy Cruzan had a quarrel with her husband at a country-music bar in Missouri. She left him there and headed for home. On the way, her car went off the road and overturned, and Nancy was thrown from the car into a ditch.

By the time EMTs arrived, she had stopped breathing for at least twelve minutes. Her heart and lungs responded to CPR, but her brain had gone too long without oxygen. She was left in a persistent vegetative state.

At a hospital, tubes were implanted in Nancy's stomach to provide food and water. Ten months later, she was transferred to a nursing home. Then Nancy's husband divorced her, and her parents, Joe and Joyce Cruzan, became her legal guardians.

In 1987, Nancy's parents decided that she should be allowed to die. So they asked the nursing home to remove the feeding tube, but the staff refused.

Nancy's parents did not have enough money to

pay an attorney for the time it would take to move the case through the lower courts. A right to die group, Society for the Right to Die, came to their aid. The lawyer they supplied, William Colby, filed suit against the nursing home.

Cruzan v. *Harmon*

In the trial court, Judge Charles Teel sided with Nancy Cruzan's parents, and the state of Missouri appealed. In 1989, when the case reached the Missouri Supreme Court, it was known as *Cruzan v. Harmon*.

The Missouri Supreme Court sided with the state. The justices demanded clear and convincing evidence of Nancy's wishes, and the testimony of Nancy's parents did not supply that evidence, they ruled. Nor had Nancy made out a living will stating her wishes.

But more importantly, the Missouri justices' ruling rested on the facts that Nancy was legally alive and not terminally ill. "The state's relevant interest is in life, both its preservation and its sanctity [holiness]. Nancy is not dead. Her life expectancy is [another] thirty years."[1] And, the justices wrote, "We do not believe her right to refuse treatment, whether that right proceeds from a constitutional right of privacy or a common law right to refuse treatment, outweighs the immense,

Legal Terms

amicus curiae—A Latin phrase meaning "friend of the court." Organizations with an interest in a case, but not directly involved, file amicus curiae briefs, stating their opinions, in an attempt to influence the court's final ruling.

appellant or petitioner—In an appeals case, the party that asks the court to reverse the lower court decision.

appellate court (also called court of appeals)—A court that reviews decisions of lower courts for fairness and accuracy. An appellate court can reverse a lower court's ruling.

appellee or respondent—In an appeals case, the party that won the lower court case and asks that the decision stand as is.

brief—A written statement of a party's argument on one or more issues in the case.

majority opinion—The U.S. Supreme Court's final ruling in a case and the reasoning behind it. **Concurring opinions** are written by justices who agree with the majority opinion but have a different path of legal reasoning. **Dissenting opinions** are written by justices who disagree with the ruling.

oral argument—An opportunity for the parties in a legal action to discuss their case with the court. Lawyers answer questions from the court and explain why their side should win.

precedent—A legal holding that will determine how courts decide in future cases.

clear fact of life in which the state maintains a vital interest. . . ."[2]

Cruzan v. Missouri

The Cruzans' lawyer appealed the Missouri Supreme Court's decision to the U.S. Supreme Court, the highest court in the land. In their appeal, the Cruzans claimed that the Missouri Supreme Court's ruling violated Nancy's constitutional right not to be subjected to unwanted medical treatment.

Cruzan v. *Missouri* began with oral arguments. Attorneys for the Cruzans and for the state of Missouri presented their cases to the nine justices. In Supreme Court cases, no witnesses are called. Only the attorneys for both sides testify. The justices stopped the attorneys from time to time to ask probing questions. This back-and-forth question-and-answer format helps the justices to understand exactly what each side has in mind.

The nine justices then began a months-long process of coming to a decision on the case and writing the ruling. The justices had to think especially long and hard about this decision. It would set precedent for right to die cases at both lower court and U.S. Supreme Court levels for many years to come.

As part of this decision-making process, the justices studied records of past cases. They also read the many *amicus curiae* briefs from organizations supporting each side in this highly controversial case.

The Ruling

High court cases are decided by majority rule. Each of the nine justices casts a vote. The vote on *Cruzan v. Missouri* was a five-to-four split. After the vote, one of the five concurring, or agreeing, justices wrote the majority opinion, explaining their decision.

The Court announced its landmark ruling on June 25, 1990. The ruling sided with the state of Missouri, against the Cruzans. But as we know, the true importance of legal rulings is not always in who wins. It often lies in what the ruling says about the matter in general. This was true of *Cruzan v. Missouri*. The majority opinion was written by Chief Justice William Rehnquist. Separate concurring opinions were written by Justices Antonin Scalia and Sandra Day O'Connor. Justice O'Connor's opinion was to become highly influential. Let's examine the main points of the majority opinion and Justice O'Connor's opinion.

On lower court rulings. When the justices surveyed lower court cases, they saw disagreement everywhere they looked:

> ◇ New Jersey's *Quinlan* and Massachusetts's *Saikewicz* rulings allow surrogates the right

to refuse treatment for incompetent patients. New York's *Storar* and New Jersey's *Conroy* deny surrogates this right.

⬥ *Quinlan* does not demand "clear and convincing evidence" of an incompetent patient's wishes, but New York's *O'Connor* ruling does.

⬥ *Saikewicz* states that only the court should decide these end-of-life issues, but *Quinlan* says family and friends should decide them.

U.S. Supreme Court justice O'Connor summed up the lower court precedents this way: "As is

These are the nine Supreme Court justices who ruled on Cruzan v. Missouri. In a 5–4 decision, they sided with the state against the Cruzans.

evident from the Court's survey of state court decisions, . . . no national consensus [agreement] has yet emerged on the best solution for this difficult and sensitive problem."[3]

On an individual's rights versus a state's rights. Eight of the nine Supreme Court justices agreed that competent patients have the right to refuse medical treatment. The *Botsford* and *Schloendorff* rulings confirm this. And they agreed that a patient's "liberty interest" is protected under the due process clause of the Fourteenth Amendment: ". . . nor shall any State deprive any person of life, liberty or property without due process of law. . . ."

In other words, the government cannot take away a person's basic rights to life, liberty, or property, unless it is proven in court that this person has violated the law. And one of those rights is the right to refuse medical treatment.

However, this right is not absolute. It must be balanced against the state's interests in protecting and preserving life. Does the Constitution forbid the state of Missouri from demanding clear and convincing evidence of Nancy Cruzan's wishes? "We hold that it does not," Rehnquist wrote.[4]

On why the State's rights should prevail. Why do the state's interests overrule the interests of the Cruzans? One reason is because death is irreversible, Rehnquist wrote. What if, in the future, a new medical discovery were made that could bring a PVS patient back to consciousness? By allowing the patient to live on, he or she might someday benefit from such a discovery. A patient who is allowed to die could never benefit from such a discovery.

And so, the Supreme Court concluded, the state may keep Nancy Cruzan alive because of its own legitimate interests in preserving and protecting human life.

Limits of the Ruling

Chief Justice Rehnquist and Justice O'Connor took care to define the limits of the majority ruling. Here are their key points.

On a constitutionally guaranteed right to die. Chief Justice Rehnquist wrote that the ruling does not answer a key question: Does the U.S. Constitution guarantee people a right to die? This is still an open question. At some time in the future, the high court may address the issue again and come to a different conclusion.

On clear and convincing evidence. Justice O'Connor said the ruling does not permanently settle the matter of clear and convincing evidence. In the future, the Court may change its mind and rule that a state must carry out the wishes of surrogates such as the Cruzans.

Influence of the Ruling

Perhaps the most important effect of *Cruzan v. Missouri* (1990) was what it accomplished in terms of public awareness. Not since *In re Quinlan* (1976) had the right to die received such nationwide attention. Suddenly, right to die issues were on a lot of people's minds.

High on the list of issues was that of advance directives. In her concurring opinion, Justice O'Connor wrote, "Few individuals provide explicit oral or written instructions regarding their intent to refuse medical treatment should they become incompetent."[5] And living wills often are not explicit enough to make the patient's wishes clear. States could help, she wrote, by passing laws allowing health-care proxies. Then, living individuals, such as a lawyer or family members, would be available to help make an incompetent patient's wishes clear.

The opinion of Justice Sandra Day O'Connor spurred new state laws legalizing health-care proxies. Her opinion also affected how states handle the tube-feeding issue. She wrote that tube feeding was an extraordinary medical procedure, and so a patient should have the right to refuse it. This spurred some states to alter laws to allow patients to refuse tube feeding, along with other life-support measures.

Aftermath

In August 1990, two months after the ruling, the Cruzans presented a Missouri court with new evidence of Nancy's wishes. Three more friends testified that Nancy had told them she would never want to be kept alive under these circumstances. Meanwhile, a public opinion poll taken shortly after the *Cruzan* v. *Missouri* ruling showed that 89 percent of Missourians would also not want to go on living if they were in Nancy's place.[6]

In light of overwhelming public opinion and this new evidence, the state did not challenge the Cruzans' request this time. Judge Charles Teel, the original trial judge, ordered the feeding tube removed. On December 26, 1990, the order was carried out. Twelve days later, and seven years after the accident that plunged her into PVS, Nancy Cruzan died.

Physician-Assisted Suicide

The next time the U.S. Supreme Court addressed a right to die issue was 1997. This time it was two similar cases decided together. Like *Cruzan*, these cases arrived at the high court on appeal after moving through the lower courts. The issue this time was physician-assisted suicide.

The cases were *Washington* v. *Glucksberg* and *Vacco* v. *Quill*. In both cases, the respondents in the lower courts included doctors and terminally ill patients. The respondents were challenging the states of Washington and New York, claiming that their state laws against PAS were unconstitutional. The two laws are virtually identical. The Washington version reads, "A person is guilty of promoting a suicide attempt when he knowingly causes or aids another person to attempt suicide."[7]

The respondents in the *Washington* case based their arguments on a point of law that the Cruzans also had used. They claimed that the Washington statute violated their liberty interest as stated in the due process clause of the Fourteenth Amendment.

The *Vacco* respondents relied on a different part of the Fourteenth Amendment, the equal protection clause, which guarantees all citizens "the equal protection of the laws."

U.S. Supreme Court Rulings

Both groups of respondents had won their lower-court cases. As a result, the Washington and New York state laws against PAS were struck down. Now the states of Washington and New York were appealing those decisions before the U.S. Supreme Court. They wanted the statutes outlawing PAS put back on the books.

On June 26, 1997, the nine justices announced their rulings. They reversed both lower-court decisions by a nine-to-zero vote. The Washington and New York state laws banning PAS were not unconstitutional, they said. Chief Justice Rehnquist, who wrote the *Cruzan* majority opinion, also wrote these opinions. Here are the key points.

On the due process clause. In the *Washington* ruling, Chief Justice Rehnquist stated, "Anglo American common law has punished or otherwise disapproved of assisting suicide for over 700 years. . . ." Why? The reasons are based on government interests in preserving and protecting life. Among these interests are "maintaining physicians' role as their patients' healers" and "protecting the poor, the elderly, disabled persons, and the terminally ill . . . from indifference, prejudice, and psychological and financial pressure to end their lives. . . ." And so, he said, "This Court's decisions lead to the conclusion that respondents' asserted 'right' to assistance in committing suicide is not a fundamental liberty interest protected by the Due Process Clause."[8]

On the equal protection clause. In the *Vacco* ruling, the Court found that the ban on assisted suicide does not violate the equal protection clause of the Fourteenth Amendment. New York's ban does not deny the disabled and terminally ill equal protection. Instead, it shields them from prejudice that might end their lives.

Limits of the Rulings

As in *Cruzan*, the *Washington* and *Vacco* rulings did not address PAS or other right to die issues on a nationwide basis. The Court ruled only that the New York and Washington state laws banning PAS were not unconstitutional. The Court left it up to individual states to deal with these issues. The Court did say that it was willing to address these issues in the future, though, if the states could not do the job.

How are the states coping now with right to die issues? The next chapter tells us.

chapter 8

The Issues Today

When we look at right to die issues at the present time, we see an overall trend toward support among lawmakers, the courts, and the public for the right to choose to die. But we also see a great deal of continued resistance. Both supporters and opponents may see things as going their way, depending on which issue they focus on. Let's look at these one by one.

Physician-Assisted Suicide

Supporters can point to Oregon, where Measure 16 remains in effect despite opponents' ongoing legal challenges. How many terminally ill people in Oregon have met the requirements to receive PAS? From 1998 through 2003, 171 patients with terminal illnesses legally took their own lives using

The Issues Today

lethal medication. Ann Jackson, executive director of the Oregon Hospice Association, said, "We estimate that one out of 100 individuals who begin the process of asking about assisted suicide will carry it out."[1] For the rest, supporters say, the drugs are a comfort, a way out if life becomes too much to bear.

On the other hand, right to die opponents can point to the rest of the nation. Bills to legalize PAS have been drawn up in several states, including Hawaii, Arizona, Vermont, and Wisconsin; but none of these bills has become law. As of 2004, Oregon remains the only state in the nation where PAS is legal.

Jack Kevorkian, sometimes known as Dr. Death, who helped some 130 people commit suicide, is serving a ten- to twenty-five-year sentence. His appeal to the U.S. Supreme Court for review of his case was turned down.

Elizabeth Bouvia

After Bouvia won her 1986 case, people expected her to take her own life by starvation. After all, she had fought for this right for years.

Instead, she chose to live on. But she remained an outspoken advocate for the right to die. In a 2002 interview, she said: "No sane person (terminal or otherwise) wishes to die." However, she added, "I hope each day that, before I have to endure continued excruciating pain and constant suffering, I will slip away as naturally and as peacefully as possible."[2]

Notice the mixed message here. She finds her life so painful that she looks forward to ending it, yet she lives on because she believes it is the sane thing to do. Her actions and words both speak loudly for the enduring human instinct to live.

PVS Patients and the Right to Die

State legislatures continue to pass laws in regard to passive euthanasia of PVS patients. In passive euthanasia, care and treatment, including nutrition and hydration, are withheld, and the patient is allowed to die. As we know, all fifty states have living-will and health-care proxy laws on the books. And many states have included tube feeding among the medical treatments that surrogates may refuse on behalf of PVS patients.

Let's look at a current case that involves all these PVS issues. One February night in 1990 in St. Petersburg, Florida, Terri Schiavo's heart stopped for several minutes. Doctors still do not know why. Terri was twenty-six when a lack of oxygen to her brain left her in PVS. She could breathe on her own, but the hospital staff had to feed her through a tube. Later, she was transferred to a Tampa Bay area hospice.

The Issues Today

Terri had not made out a living will. But her husband and legal guardian, Michael, said he knew what she would want. Several times in the past, he said, she had told him she would not want to be kept alive artificially. Michael Schiavo wanted the feeding tube withdrawn so that Terri could die.

But Terri's parents, Bob and Mary Schindler, wanted her to live. They insisted that one day, with the proper care, their daughter could recover at least some of her physical and mental abilities.

Six years of legal battles followed. Court-appointed doctors found that Terri Schiavo was in a persistent vegetative state. The noises and facial expressions she made were only reflex actions, they testified. The courts kept siding with Michael Schiavo, and Bob and Mary Schindler kept on appealing. Finally, in June 2003, Florida's Second District Court ruled in Michael Schiavo's favor, and the Florida Supreme Court refused to overturn the ruling.

The situation appeared to be settled on October 15, 2003, when doctors removed the feeding tube. However, Florida lawmakers stepped in. The state legislature passed an emergency law allowing the staff at the hospice where Terri was being cared for to reinsert the feeding tube. The court battles continue, and Terri Schiavo continues to live on in a persistent vegetative state.

Significance of the Ruling

Like *Quinlan* and *Cruzan*, the Schiavo case drew national attention. Opposition was strong. Florida governor Jeb Bush said he received twenty-seven thousand e-mails asking him to intervene in the case.[3] Christian right-to-life groups and disability-rights groups spoke out against removal. Max Lapertosa is an attorney representing disability organizations. He said, "The law shouldn't judge some lives as worthless. That's a very disturbing thought to a lot of families who have sons and daughters with severe disabilities."[4]

Author and attorney Wesley Smith, a prominent

A demonstrator sits with a picture of Terri Schiavo as part of a protest to urge the governor of Florida to intervene in the controversial case.

right to die opponent, would agree with Lapertosa. He wrote:

> In our society today, because of this right to die advocacy and the idea that it isn't the *sanctity* of human life that counts but the *quality* of human life, the benefit of doubt is being moved towards the side of death.[5]

When we look back on the right to die cases since *Quinlan* (1976), Smith's conclusion seems correct. On the whole, right to die supporters would say that progress is being made, while opponents would say that things are getting worse.

In Years to Come

Scientists continue to find new ways to help us live longer, healthier lives. During the last century, their efforts helped raise our life expectancy in the United States from age forty-seven to age seventy-seven, and this upward trend continues. Look at these facts and predictions about living longer, gathered from the U.S. Census Bureau:

- ◇ During the 1990s, the number of people over age eighty-five increased by 38 percent.[6]
- ◇ Between 1990 and 2020, the number of people between sixty-five and seventy-four is expected to grow by 74 percent, while the population under sixty-five should grow by only 24 percent.[7]

Cruzan v. Missouri *and the Right to Die Debate*

⋄ By the year 2030, about one in five Americans will be age sixty-five or older.[8]

With so many more people living so much longer, courts are likely to spend more time on right to die issues in years to come. And the public, along with the media, is likely to spend more time debating these issues. Chief Justice Rehnquist ended his majority opinion in the *Washington* case this way:

> Throughout the Nation, Americans are engaged in an earnest and profound debate about the morality, legality and practicality of physician assisted suicide. Our holding permits this debate to continue, as it should in a democratic society.[9]

The next chapter shows how you can participate in this right to die debate.

chapter 9

Moot Court: Your Turn to Debate

The next step beyond reading about judicial cases is holding a mock court proceeding of your own. One type is called "moot court." Moot court is a dramatization of a hypothetical (fictitious) case or an actual case that went before an appeals court or the Supreme Court. The purpose of these courts is to rule on a lower court's decision. It is different from the criminal trial—no witnesses are called in a moot court, for example, just as no witnesses are called in a Supreme Court case. Also, the focus is on whether the court below made any mistakes rather than on finding the facts in a case.

In moot court, the players take the roles of justices, clerks, attorneys, and journalists. They

Cruzan v. Missouri *and the Right to Die Debate*

do research, write briefs, and argue legal issues before a make-believe panel of appeals court judges. The exercise hones research, writing, and debate skills.

Taking part in a moot court is a fun way to get a feeling for how a real court case occurs. Try a moot court activity with your class or club. Here's how.[1]

Step 1: Assign Roles

Here are the roles you will need to fill:

- ◇ Nine justices. They hear the attorneys' arguments, question them, and then write and deliver the final ruling: the majority opinion. Individual justices may choose to issue concurring or dissenting opinions of their own. One person is chosen to be Chief Justice, who directs the trial. Review chapter 7 for how justices do their part.

- ◇ Two or more court clerks. They work with the justices to prepare questions to ask the attorneys during oral arguments.

- ◇ A team of two or more attorneys for the petitioners, or appellants. They argue the case for the Cruzans.

- ◇ A team of two or more attorneys for the respondents, or appellees. They argue the case for the state of Missouri and the nursing home.

- ◇ Each team has a designated spokesperson to present the argument, but any of the attorneys can respond to questions from the justices. Attorneys must address the major issues by giving the most persuasive arguments for their side. Review chapters 3, 4, and 7 for help here.

- ◇ Two or more reporters. They interview the attorneys before the case and write news stories about the facts of the case and the final ruling.
- ◇ The bailiff, who calls the Court to order.

Step 2: Prepare for the Hearing

Part 1: Gather Information

The role-players must become familiar with

- ◇ *Cruzan v. Missouri*;
- ◇ *Cruzan v. Harmon*;
- ◇ other right to die cases cited as precedent by the Court, such as *In re Quinlan*.

See chapters 6 and 7 for the basic facts on these cases. More detailed information, such as transcripts of hearings and trials, is available on the Internet.

One more source of information is experts from your community, such as the following:

- ◇ A bioethics committee. Most big-city hospitals have committees of physicians, nurses, social workers, and other experts to help make end-of-life decisions in PVS and other difficult cases.

- ◆ A hospice official. A hospice organization may have someone who could offer background on end-of-life decisions.
- ◆ An attorney. Some handle end-of-life cases or know of attorneys who do.
- ◆ An advocate group. Officials from right-to-die, right-to-life, or disability-rights groups might agree to discuss their group's point of view on the case.

Part 2: Write Your Briefs

A legal brief is a written presentation of your argument. Brainstorm with the lawyers on your team. Which arguments are strongest for you? What are your weaknesses?

You may want to divide up arguments for research and writing. If so, be sure to work as a team to put the brief together. Otherwise, your brief may have holes or read poorly.

The text of the brief should have these sections:

A. Statement of the issue for review: What question is before the Court?

B. Statement of the case: What is this case about? How did the trial court rule?

C. Statement of the facts: Briefly describe the facts relevant to the case.

D. Summary of the argument: Sum up your argument in 150 words or less.

E. Argument: Spell out the legal arguments that support your side. You can split this into sections with subheadings for each part. Include references to cases or authorities that help your side.

F. Conclusion: Ask the court to rule for your client.

Real appeals briefs may be thirty pages long. Limit your brief to no more than five typed pages, double-spaced, or about 1,250 words. If possible, type on a computer. Otherwise, write very neatly.

On an agreed-upon date, each team gives the other side a copy of its brief. Each judge gets a copy too. If you do this in class, give the teacher a copy. Be sure each team member keeps a copy of the brief too.

In real life, lawyers often prepare reply briefs. They answer points made by the other side. You won't do that. But you should be ready to answer their points in oral argument.

Part 3: Prepare for Oral Argument

Judges should read all the briefs before oral argument. They should prepare questions for the lawyers.

Each side will have up to fifteen minutes to argue its case. Lawyers on each team may divide their time among speakers. Practice your arguments together!

Don't get flustered if a judge interrupts with a question. Answer the question honestly. Then move on.

Cruzan v. Missouri and the Right to Die Debate

Step 3: Hold the Hearing

Part 1: Assemble the Participants

- ◇ The justices sit together in the front of the room. This is the bench. They should not enter until the bailiff calls the Court to order. A speaking podium or lectern faces the bench.

- ◇ The petitioners' team of attorneys sits at one side, facing the justices.

- ◇ The respondents' team sits at the opposite side, also facing the justices.

- ◇ The reporters sit at the back.

- ◇ As the justices enter, the bailiff calls the Court to order: "Oyez (oy-yay)! Oyez! Oyez! The Supreme Court of the United States is now in session with the Honorable Chief Justice _____ presiding. All will stand and remain standing until the justices are seated and the Chief Justice has asked all present to be seated."

Part 2: Present the Case

- ◇ The Chief Justice calls the case and asks whether the parties are ready. Each team's spokesperson answers, "Yes."

- ◇ The appellants' spokesperson approaches the podium saying, "May it please the Court." Then the argument begins. Justices interrupt when they wish to ask a question. The attorneys respectfully answer any questions as asked.

Moot Court: Your Turn to Debate

- ◈ Then the appellees' team takes its turn. Each team has an agreed-upon time limit to present its argument.
- ◈ After the arguments, the bailiff tells everyone to rise as the justices leave to make their decision.
- ◈ After an agreed-upon time limit, the justices return and present their ruling, announced by the Chief Justice.

Part 3: Publish and Report

- ◈ A few days later, the Court's majority opinion is made available in written form, along with any dissenting opinions and individual concurring opinions.
- ◈ At the same time, the reporters' stories are made available.

Questions for Discussion

1. Do you think Elizabeth Bouvia should be allowed to starve herself in the hospital? What about the doctors and nurses who work in the hospital—do they have the right to refuse to follow her wishes?

2. Some disabled people oppose physician-assisted suicide, while others support it. What are some reasons why people in each group might feel the way they do?

3. Do you think that Dr. Jack Kevorkian should have been convicted for helping other people to die? Why or why not?

4. Can you think of other issues in which the slippery-slope argument is used? Do you think it is a good argument?

5. Do some research into Oregon's Death With Dignity law. What have been some of its effects?

6. What impact has technology had on the issue of the right to die?

7. If a terminally ill or severely disabled person cannot make medical decisions, who do you think should have the right to decide about giving or withholding treatment?

Questions for Discussion

8. Do you think there is a moral difference between providing a person with medication or surgery and providing a person with a respirator or feeding tube? Why or why not?

9. If you were in a persistent vegetative state, would you want to go on living? Why or why not?

Chronology

400 B.C.—Hippocrates issues his Hippocratic Oath, pledging that a physician's foremost duties are to heal patients and never to harm them.

1890—Scientists develop a vaccine that successfully prevents diphtheria.

1891—*Union Pacific Railway Co. v. Botsford*. The U.S. Supreme Court rules that a person has the right to refuse medical treatment.

1914—*Mary E. Schloendorff v. The Society of the New York Hospital*. The Court of Appeals of New York strongly affirms *Botsford*.

1927—The first successful respirator is developed.

1954—The first successful human organ transplant is performed.

1970s—A patients'-rights movement develops, challenging the power of the state and of doctors to dictate end-of-life treatment for patients.

1973—*Roe v. Wade*. U.S. Supreme Court upholds a woman's right to choose to terminate a pregnancy and legalizes abortion in all fifty states.

1973—The American Hospital Association develops a patient's bill of rights, outlining the doctrine of

Chronology

informed consent, which makes health-care facilities responsible for seeing that patients make informed decisions about health care.

1976—*In re Quinlan.* The New Jersey Supreme Court rules that PVS patient Karen Ann Quinlan may be unhooked from a respirator, in line with the substituted judgment wishes of her parents. Karen lives on until 1985.

1976—The California Natural Death Act is passed. This marks the first time a state has passed laws about making living wills legal and protecting physicians from being sued for not allowing terminally ill patients to die. Ten more states pass similar laws the same year.

1980—The Catholic Church issues a declaration in favor of allowing terminally ill patients to refuse extraordinary life support measures, and against physician-assisted suicide.

1982—Infant Doe, a severely handicapped infant, dies after an Indiana court permits his parents to deny him medical treatment.

1986—*Bouvia v. Superior Court.* The California Court of Appeal rules that Elizabeth Bouvia may die by starvation while under medical care. But she decides to live on instead.

1989—The U.S. Civil Rights Commission issues a

report strongly criticizing the view that severely handicapped infants should be allowed to die.

1990—*Cruzan* v. *Missouri*. In its first right to die case, the U.S. Supreme Court rules, 5–4, that a Missouri nursing home does not have to disconnect a feeding tube from PVS patient Nancy Cruzan. The Court makes a point of stating that the U.S. Constitution does not guarantee citizens a right to choose to die.

1991—The federal Patient Self-Determination Act (PSDA) becomes effective, requiring all health-care facilities that receive Medicare or Medicaid funds to inform patients of their right to refuse medical treatment and to sign advance directives.

1994—All fifty states and the District of Columbia now recognize some type of advance directive.

1997—*Washington* v. *Glucksberg* and *Vacco* v. *Quill*. The U.S. Supreme Court unanimously reverses lower court decisions in Washington state and New York state. The Court's ruling lets stand state laws that make physician-assisted suicide a crime.

1997—Measure 16 goes into effect, making Oregon the first state to legalize physician-assisted suicide. As of 2004, it remains the only state where PAS is legal.

Chronology

1999—A Michigan court sentences Jack Kevorkian, who has assisted some 130 patients in committing suicide, to ten to twenty-five years in prison for committing active euthanasia.

2003—The Florida state legislature passes an emergency law that allows a nursing home to reinsert a feeding and hydration tube into Terri Schiavo, who has been in PVS since 1990. Schiavo's husband wants the tube unhooked so that she may be allowed to die. Her parents oppose the move. More legal battles follow.

Chapter Notes

Chapter 1. Legal Questions: The Case of Elizabeth Bouvia

1. Derek Humphry and Ann Wickett, *The Right to Die: Understanding Euthanasia* (New York: Harper & Row, 1986), p. 150.

2. Mary Johnson, "Right to Life, Fight to Die: The Elizabeth Bouvia saga," *Electric Edge*, January/February 1997, <http://www.normemma.com/ebouvia.htm> (August 1, 2004).

3. Humphry and Wickett, p. 158.

4. Cited in *Bouvia v. Superior Court (Glenchur) (1986) 179 Cal.App.3d 1127, 225 Cal.Rptr. 297*, n.d., <http://login.findlaw.com/scripts/callaw?dest=ca/calapp3d/179/1127.html> (September 12, 2003).

5. Ibid.

6. "US hospitals in dilemma over vegetative patients," *Catholic News*, April 13, 2004, <www.cathnews.com/news/ 404/52.php> (September 1, 2004).

Chapter 2. The Changing Face of Death

1. *Union Pacific Railway Co. v. Botsford 141 US 250*. Supreme Court of the United States (1891). Cited in *Cruzan v. Director, MDH 497 U.S. 261*. Supreme Court of the United States (1990), <http://caselaw.lp.findlaw.com/scripts/getcase.pl?court=us&vol=497&invol=261> (August 11, 2003).

2. *Mary E. Schloendorff, Appellant, v. The Society of the New York Hospital*, Respondent. Court of Appeals of New York, 1914, <http://wings.buffalo.edu/faculty/research/bioethics/schloen1.html> (August 11, 2003).

3. "National Polling on Physician Assisted Dying," *Death with Dignity*, n.d., <http://www.deathwithdignity.org/resources/polls.htm> (July 16, 2003).

Chapter 3. Through Supporters' Eyes

1. Liz Kowalczyk, "Rationing of medical care under study," *boston.com*, September 14, 2003, <http://www.boston.com/news/local/articles/2003/09/14/rationing_of_medical_care_under_study?mode=PF> (September 1, 2004).

2. Ron Panzer, "When Will Prosecutors Act?" *Hospice Patients Alliance*, July 12, 2000, <http://www.hospicepatients.org/when-will-prosecutors-act.html> (July 30, 2004).

3. Peter Singer, *Rethinking Life and Death: The Collapse of Our Traditional Ethics* (New York: St. Martin's Press, 1995), p. 219.

4. Nancy Gibbs, "Love and Let Die," *Time*, March 19, 1990, p. 67.

5. Diane Coleman, "Assisted Suicide and Disability: Another Perspective," *Human Rights*, Winter 2000, <http://www.abanet.org/irr/hr/winter00humanrights/colemand.html> (August 12, 2004).

Chapter 4. Through Opponents' Eyes

1. "Florida Bishops Urge Safer Course for Terri Schiavo," Florida Catholic Conference, August 27, 2003, <http://www.flacathconf.org/Publications/BishopsStatements/Bpst2000/TerriSchiavo.htm> (July 30, 2004).

2. Nancy Gibbs, "Love and Let Die," *Time*, March 19, 1990, p. 65.

Chapter Notes

3. Franjo Cardinal Seper, Prefect, "Sacred Congregation for the Doctrine of the Faith: Declaration on Euthanasia, Vatican, May 5, 1980," *Euthanasia.com*, <http://www.euthanasia.com/vatican.html> (July 30, 2004).

4. Daniel Callahan, *The Troubled Dream of Life: Living with Mortality* (New York: Simon & Schuster, 1993), pp. 81–82.

5. William G. Most, "Problems of Artificial Feeding," *The Catholic Resource Network*, 1994, <http://www.ewtn.com/library/ISSUES/FEEDING.TXT> (July 30, 2004).

6. "Statement of Bishop Robert N. Lynch concerning the Terri Schiavo case," Florida Catholic Conference, August 12, 2003, <http://www.dioceseofstpete.org/news_releases/statement_of_bishop_robert_n.htm> (November 12, 2004).

7. Ibid.

8. Derek Humphry and Ann Wickett, *The Right to Die: Understanding Euthanasia* (New York: Harper & Row, 1986), p. 166.

9. "Euthanasia: Advance Legal Directives," *Ohio Right to Life*, <http://www.ohiolife.org/euthanasia/advancedir.asp> (September 22, 2003).

10. Hippocrates, translated by Francis Adams, "The Oath," *The Internet Classics Archive*, n.d., <http://classics.mit.edu/Hippocrates/hippooath.html> (August 27, 2003).

11. Kim MacQueen, "Last Wish: The Rise of the Right to Die," *Research in Review*, Winter 1993, <http://mailer.fsu.edu/~research/RinR/Final.html> (August 1, 2004).

12. "E-2.211 Physician-Assisted Suicide," *American Medical Association*, June 1994, <http://www.ama-assn.org/ama/pub/category/8459.html> (August 1, 2004).

13. Gibbs, p. 66.

14. Arthur J. Dyke, *Life's Worth: The Case Against Assisted Suicide* (excerpt), The Center for Bioethics and Human Dignity, December 3, 2002, <http://www.cbhd.org/resources/endoflife/dyck_2002-12-03.htm> (August 1, 2004).

15. Seper.

16. "Position Statement on Physician-Assisted Suicide," *Hawaii Right to Life*, n.d., <http://www.hpacc.org/positions/hrtl.php> (September 22, 2003).

17. Peter G. Filene, *In the Arms of Others: A Cultural History of the Right-to-Die in America* (Chicago: I. R. Dee, 1998), pp. 216–217.

18. R. M. Dworkin, *Freedom's Law: The Moral Reading of the American Constitution* (Cambridge, Mass.: Harvard University Press, 1996), p. 145.

19. Matt Ridley, *Genome: The Autobiography of a Species in 23 Chapters* (New York: HarperCollins, 2000), p. 290.

20. Rob Jonquiere, "Van de Wal/Van der Maas report," May 7, 2004, <http://www.nvve.nl/english/info/remmelinkreport23-05-03.htm> (September 1, 2004).

21. Paul F. Stavis, "Newborns with Significant Handicaps: What is their right to be medically treated or to have treatment refused? And, who oversees it?" New York State Commission on Quality of Care, January–February 1990, <http://www.cqc.state.ny.us/counsels_corner/cc43.htm#back1> (September 1, 2004).

Chapter Notes

22. Diane Coleman, "Assisted Suicide and Disability: Another Perspective," *Human Rights*, Winter 2000, <http://www.abanet.org/irr/hr/winter00humanrights/colemand.html> (August 12, 2004).

23. "Death and Dignity," *The Nation*, February 3, 1997, p. 3.

24. Coleman.

Chapter 5. Right to Die Laws

1. *Union Pacific Railway Co. v. Botsford 141 US 250*. Supreme Court of the United States (1891). Cited in *Cruzan v. Director, MDH 497 U.S. 261*. Supreme Court of the United States (1990), <http://caselaw.lp.findlaw.com/scripts/getcase.pl?court=us&vol=497&invol=261> (November 15, 2004).

2. Robert Bunting and Joyce Benton, "Advance Directives: What Every Nurse Needs to Know." *The Journal of Nursing Risk Management 2000*, Armed Forces Institute of Pathology, n.d., <http://www.afip.org/Departments/legalmed/jnrm2000/ directives.htm> (June 22, 2004).

3. Denise Grady, "At Life's End, Many Patients Are Denied Peaceful Passing," *Multiple Sclerosis News*, May 29, 2000, <http://www.mult-sclerosis.org/news/May2000/PlanningforDeathPt1.html> (August 1, 2004).

4. Derek Humphry, "Assisted Suicide Laws Around the World," *Assisted Suicide*, September 18, 2003, <http://www.assistedsuicide.org/suicide_laws.html> (August 1, 2004).

5. Jeffrey Rosen, "What Right to Die?" *New Republic*, June 24, 1996, p. 31.

6. "Jack Kevorkian: Assisted-Suicide Pioneer," *abcnews.com*, n.d., <http://abcnews.go.com/reference/bios/kevorkian.html> (August 1, 2004).

7. Ibid.

Chapter 6. Lower Court Cases

1. Peter G. Filene, *In the Arms of Others: A Cultural History of the Right-to-Die in America* (Chicago: I. R. Dee, 1998), p. 19.

2. "Matter of Quinlan (excerpts) 70 N.J. 10(1976) – Supreme Court of New Jersey," n.d., <http://www.csulb.edu/~jvancamp/452_r6.html> (August 1, 2004).

3. Filene, p. 93.

4. Ibid., p. 146.

Chapter 7. U.S. Supreme Court Cases

1. "*Cruzan v. Harmon* (excerpts) 760 SW2d 408 (1988)—Supreme Court of Missouri," n.d., <http://www.csulb.edu/~jvancamp/452_r7.html> (August 1, 2004).

2. Ibid.

3. Justice Sandra Day O'Connor, "881503CONCUR v. DIRECTOR, MISSOURI DEPT. OF HEALTH," n.d., <http://supct.law.cornell.edu/supct/html/88-1503.ZC1.html> (November 15, 2004).

4. Chief Justice William Rehnquist, "881503OPINION V. DIRECTOR, MISSOURI DEPT. OF HEALTH," n.d., <http://supct.law.cornell.edu/supct/html/88-1503.ZO.html> (August 1, 2004).

5. O'Connor.

6. Peter G. Filene, *In the Arms of Others: A Cultural History of the Right-to-Die in America* (Chicago: I. R. Dee, 1998), p. 182.

Chapter Notes

7. "Chronology of Lawsuits: The Constitutional Challenges to State Laws Regarding End of Life Decisions," *Compassion in Dying Federation*, n.d., <http://www.compassionindying.org/legal/cidconst.html> (August 12, 2003).

8. Syllabus, *Washington et al. v. Glucksberg et al.* No. 96-110. Supreme Court of the United States, June 26, 1997, <http://supct.law.cornell.edu/supct/html/96-110.ZS.html> (August 1, 2004).

Chapter 8. The Issues Today

1. "Ashcroft earns rebuff by U.S. appeals court," *Tri-CityHerald.com*, June 3, 2004, <http://www.tri-cityherald.com/tch/opinions/story/5150832p-5083054c.html> (August 1, 2004).

2. "Does Choice = Push?: Reviewing a Landmark Court Case," interview with Elizabeth Bouvia by Dr. Faye Girsh, *The Hemlock Society USA*, September 30, 2002, <http://www.hemlock.org/News/EditNews.asp?NewsID=57> (October 12, 2003).

3. Associated Press, "Jeb Bush Intervenes in Coma Case," *CBSNews.com*, August 27, 2003, <http://www.cbsnews.com/stories/2003/08/27/health/main570303.shtml> (August 2, 2004).

4. Maya Bell, "Parents Have Exhausted Appeals in Daughter's Case," *Orlando Sentinel*, September 10, 2003, p. B1.

5. Sarah Foster, "Attorney: Jeb Bush letter only a 'good first step,'" *WorldNetDaily*, August 28, 2003, <http://worldnetdaily.com/news/printer-friendly.asp?ARTICLE_ID=34321> (August 2, 2004).

6. "The 65 Years and Over Population: 2000," *United States Census 2000*, n.d., <http://www.census.gov/prod/2001pubs/c2kbr01-10.pdf> (June 22, 2004).

7. "Aging in the United States—Past, Present, and Future," *U.S. Department of Commerce, National Institute on Aging*, n.d., <http://www.census.gov/ipc/prod/97agewc.pdf> (June 22, 2004).

8. Ibid.

9. "Chronology of Lawsuits: The Constitutional Challenges to State Laws Regarding End of Life Decisions," *Compassion in Dying Federation*, n.d., <http://www.compassionindying.org/legal/cidconst.html> (August 12, 2003).

Chapter 9. Moot Court: Your Turn to Debate

1. Adapted from Millie Aulbur, "Constitutional Issues and Teenagers," *The Missouri Bar*, n.d., <http://www.mobar.org/teach/cleasson.htm> (December 10, 2004); Street Law Inc. and The Supreme Court Historical Society, "Moot Court Activity," 2002, <http://www.landmarkcases.org> (December 10, 2004); with suggestions from Kathiann M. Kowalski.

Glossary

advance directive—A legal document stating a person's end-of-life wishes if he or she ever becomes incompetent. Living wills and health-care proxies are the two chief kinds of advance directives. A living will states a person's wishes in writing. A health-care proxy, also known as a durable health-care power of attorney, designates another person to assist in explaining a patient's living will to physicians.

autonomy—The freedom to determine for yourself what you will do or how you will behave.

bioethics—The study of moral and ethical problems that arise because of scientific advances, such as life support treatments.

competent—Able to make end-of-life decisions on one's own.

doctrine of informed consent—A procedure by which physicians inform patients of how they plan to treat them and the risks involved, and patients then consent to or refuse that treatment.

doctrine of substituted judgment—A procedure by which a surrogate, often a guardian, is allowed to make end-of-life medical decisions for an incompetent patient.

durable health care power of attorney—See *advance directive.*

eugenics—A social movement with the goal of improving the human race by selective breeding. In practice, this has led to the sterilization and killing of people classified as "inferior," including people who are severely handicapped or severely mentally ill.

euthanasia—A Greek word originally meaning "happy death," and now meaning the deliberate ending of a human life in as painless a manner as possible. *Active euthanasia* is the direct killing of a patient. In *passive euthanasia*, physicians give patients lethal doses of drugs but do not administer them. Or they withhold patients' life-support treatment, allowing them to die a natural death. *Voluntary euthanasia* is the killing of a patient who has requested death. *Involuntary euthanasia*, or *mercy killing*, is the killing of a patient who has not asked to die, such as a severely handicapped infant or a severely mentally ill adult. Mercy killing may also be the killing of a terminally ill adult who has asked to die in order to relieve his or her suffering.

feeding and hydration tube—A life-support treatment consisting of a tube inserted into a

Glossary

patient's stomach to supply liquid food and water directly.

guardian—A person who is legally responsible for the affairs of someone who is young or who cannot take care of his or her own affairs.

health-care proxy—See *advance directive*.

hospice—A program for terminally ill patients, designed to help them die comfortably with a minimum of pain. Most hospice workers deal with patients in their homes.

incompetent—Unable to make end-of-life decisions on one's own. PVS patients, infants, and severely mentally ill adults are incompetent.

life expectancy—The average number of years a person can be expected to live.

life support—The use of special medical treatment, such as respirators and feeding tubes, to keep alive people who otherwise would die.

living will—See *advance directive*.

mercy killing—See *euthanasia*.

persistent vegetative state (PVS)—A medical term for patients who are permanantly unconscious but technically alive. Without life-support treatment, they would die.

physician-assisted suicide (PAS)—A form of passive euthanasia in which a physician helps a terminally ill patient to die, usually by getting the patient a lethal dose of drugs that the patient administers, not the physician.

quality of life—A measure of how much people are able to enjoy living, depending on their physical and mental well-being.

respirator—A life-support machine that breathes for a patient.

right to die—The legal right to control the time, place, and manner of one's death.

slippery slope argument—The argument that a proposal is dangerous because, if put into action, it will lead to a series of increasingly negative events. Right to die opponents use this argument when speaking against legalizing physician-assisted suicide.

surrogate—A person who acts on behalf of an incompetent patient to see that the patient's wishes are fulfilled.

terminally ill—Having six months or less to live, with no hope of being cured.

whole-brain death—A condition in which a patient's entire brain, including the brain stem, has stopped operating. This is the legal standard for determining death in all fifty states.

Further Reading

Altman, Linda Jacobs. *Death: An Introduction to Medical-Ethical Dilemmas*. Berkeley Heights, N.J.: Enslow Publishers, 2000.

Balkin, Karen, editor. *Assisted Suicide*. San Diego, Calif.: Greenhaven Press, 2005.

Donelly, Karen. *Cruzan v. Missouri: The Right to Die*. New York: Rosen, 2004.

Hyde, Margaret O., and John F. Setaro. *When the Brain Dies First*. New York: Franklin Watts, 2000.

Marzilli, Alan. *Physician-Assisted Suicide*. Philadelphia: Chelsea House Publishers, 2003.

Torr, James, ed. *Euthanasia: Opposing Viewpoints*. San Diego, Calif.: Greenhaven Press, 2000.

Yount, Lisa. *Euthanasia*. San Diego, Calif.: Lucent Books, 2001.

Internet Addresses

Death With Dignity
   <http://www.dwd.org>

National Right to Life
   <http://nrlc.org>

National Hospice and Palliative Care Organization
   <http://www.nhpco.org>

Index

A

advance directives, 30–31, 42, 54–56, 85. *See also* living wills and health-care proxies.
American Academy of Neurology (AAN), 29, 39
American Civil Liberties Union (ACLU), 8
American Medical Association (AMA), 44
amicus curiae brief, 28, 29, 39–40, 79, 81
Annas, George, 44
Association of American Physicians and Surgeons, 39–40
autonomy, 20–23, 27, 31, 33, 36

B

bioethics committees, 31, 99
Boston University, 44
Botsford, Clara, 19–20
Bouvia, Elizabeth, 5–6, 7–10, 11, 35, 91–92
Bouvia v. Superior Court (1986), 9–10, 11, 15, 16
Browning, Estelle, 55
Bush, Jeb, 94

C

cardiopulmonary resuscitation (CPR), 56, 77
Cardozo, Benjamin, 21
Catholic Bishops of Florida, 38
Cohen, Sidney, 45

Colby, William, 78
common law, 52–53, 75, 78
competence, 9–11, 15, 23, 27, 31, 38, 41, 53, 72, 73, 75, 83, 85
Conroy, Claire, 71
Cooper, Jessica, 62
Cruzan, Joe and Joyce, 77–78, 80, 81, 83, 84, 86, 87, 98
Cruzan, Nancy, 12–13, 14, 15, 29, 30, 39, 56, 57, 64, 77–78, 80, 83, 84, 86
Cruzan v. Director, Missouri Department of Health. See Cruzan v. Missouri.
Cruzan v. Harmon (1989), 77, 78, 80, 99
Cruzan v. Missouri (1990), 12–15, 16, 28, 29, 39–40, 54, 64, 69, 76–78, 80–86, 88, 89, 94, 99

D

depression, 44–45
discrimination, 51
doctrine of double effect, 32
doctrine of informed consent, 23, 27, 58
doctrine of substituted judgment, 13, 30, 66, 68
Do Not Resuscitate (DNR) order, 56–57
Dr. Death. *See* Kevorkian, Jack.
Due Process Clause, 88

durable health-care power of attorney. *See* health-care proxies.

E

Eichner, Philip K., 70
Eighth Amendment, 14
equal protection clause, 88
eugenics, 47–48, 49, 66, 74
euthanasia, 47, 48
 active, 6, 35, 60
 passive, 92

F

federal laws, 53–56
feeding tubes, 8, 10, 11, 13, 15, 19, 28, 29, 40–41, 42, 49, 53, 71, 72, 73, 74, 77, 85, 86, 92, 93
Fleming, Alexander, 18
Florida Catholic Conference, 43
Fourteenth Amendment, 14, 83, 87, 88
Fox, Joseph Charles, 70, 71

G

guardians, 13, 41, 69, 70, 71, 72, 93

H

Habiger, Matthew, 47
Hawaii Right to Life, 46
health-care proxies, 42, 54, 85, 92
Hippocrates, 43
Hippocratic Oath, 43
Holmes, Oliver Wendell, 47
Horkan, Tom, 43–44
hospice, 46, 92, 93, 100
Human Life Alliance, 42
Human Life International, 47

hydration tubes, 19, 29, 40, 77

I

Infant Doe case, 49–50
In re Conroy, Supreme Court of New Jersey (1985), 71–72, 73, 74, 82
In re Cruzan. See Cruzan v. Missouri.
In re Quinlan, New Jersey Supreme Court (1976), 64–69, 73–74, 81–82, 85, 94, 95, 99
In re Storar, Court of Appeals of New York (1981), 70–71, 74
In re Westchester County Medical Center on behalf of O'Connor, Court of Appeals of New York (1988), 72–73, 74, 82
intensive care units (ICUs), 28

J

Jackson, Ann, 91

K

Kevorkian, Jack, 59–60, 62, 63, 91

L

Lapertosa, Max, 94, 95
legal brief, 100–101
liberty interest, 83, 87, 88
life expectancy, 17, 95–96
life support, 7, 11, 19, 25, 27–28, 31, 38, 40, 46, 56, 65, 67, 68, 85
living wills, 42–43, 54–55, 78, 85, 92, 93
lower court cases. *See* precedent-setting court rulings.

Index

Ludington, Pierre, 33
Lynch, Robert N., 41–42

M

Mary E. Schloendorff v. The Society of the New York Hospital (1914), 21, 83
Measure 16, 58, 90
medical proxies. *See* health-care proxies.
Mercitron machine, 59
mercy killing, 35, 74
moot court, 97–103
Morse, Robert, 65, 66, 67
Most, William G., 41
Muir, Robert, 66, 67, 68

N

nasogastric tubes. *See* feeding tubes.
National Right to Life Committee, 74
Not Dead Yet, 51

O

O'Connor, Sandra Day, 54, 81, 82–83, 84, 85
Ohio Right to Life, 42–43
opponents' view on right to die, 37–51
Oregon Death With Dignity, 58
Oregon Hospice Association, 91

P

Patient Self-Determination Act (PSDA) of 1991, 56
patients' rights movement, 20–23, 25
persistent vegetative state (PVS), 11, 12, 27–28, 29, 30, 31, 38–41, 55, 57, 65, 66, 69, 70, 77, 84, 86, 92, 93, 99
petitioners, 14
physician-assisted suicide (PAS), 6, 25, 31–35, 36, 43–47, 50, 54, 57–60, 86–89, 90–91
precedent-setting court rulings, 63–75, 78, 80, 99

Q

Quinlan, Joseph, 65
Quinlan, Karen Ann, 64–69

R

Rehnquist, William, 81, 83, 84, 88, 96
religious views, 40–42, 45–46
Remmelink report, 48
respirator, 19, 28, 40, 42, 53, 65, 68, 70
respondents, 14, 15
Roe v. Wade (1973), 22–23, 32, 53–54
Roosevelt, Theodore, 47

S

Saikewicz, Joseph, 69
Scalia, Antonin, 81
Schiavo, Michael, 93
Schiavo, Terri, 92–93
Schiavo v. Florida Supreme Court (2003), 92–94
Schindler, Bob and Mary, 93
Schloendorff, Mary, 21
Senander, Mary, 42
Singer, Peter, 33
slippery slope argument, 34–36, 46–47, 49, 66, 74
Smith, Wesley, 94–95
Society for the Right to Die, 78

state laws, 53–55, 57, 58, 65, 87, 89, 92
Storar, John, 70, 71
suicide, 6, 40, 88
Superintendent of Belchertown State School v. *Saikewicz* (1977), 69–70, 74, 81–82
supporters' views on the right to die, 26–36
surrogates, 13, 23, 66, 68, 71, 73, 74, 75, 84, 92

T

Teel, Charles, 78, 86

U

Union Pacific Railway Company v. *Botsford* (1891), 19–20, 21, 22, 53, 83

U. S. Census Bureau, 95
U. S. Civil Rights Commission, 35, 49–50

V

Vacco v. *Quill* (1997), 86–87, 88, 89

W

Washington v. *Glucksberg* (1997), 54, 58, 86–87, 88, 89, 96
whole-brain death, 57

Y

Youk, Thomas, 60